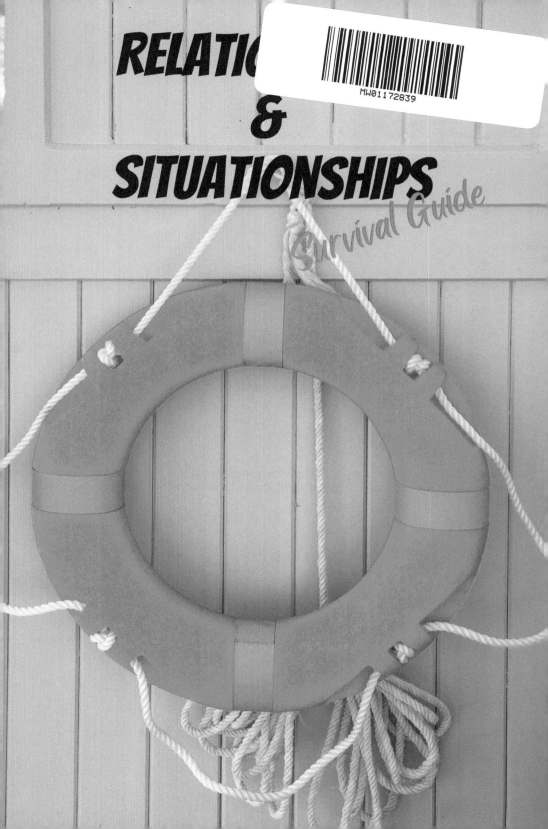

Relationships & Situationships Survival Guide Copyright © 2022 by Sonya L. Manuel

All rights reserved.

All right reserved. No part of this book may be reproduced or used in any manner without the prior written permission of the copyright owner, except for the use of brief quotations in a book review.

LWI Publishing Services

Sonya L. Manuel
Visit my website www.sonyalmanuel.com

Printed in the United States of America
First Printing: June 2022

Relationships & Situationships Survival Guide Copyright © 2022 by Sonya L. Manuel
All rights reserved.
ISBN: 979-8-9857902-2-1

DEDICATION

This book is dedicated to all who have inspired me, supported me and to anyone who has pushed through the pain of a heartbreaking relationship, lip electrolysis, or a Brazilian bikini wax because we've learned that pain is inevitable, suffering is optional, tears are acceptable.

ACKNOWLEDGMENTS

Endless thanks to my Life Coach and Mentor, the beautiful Mrs. Lisa Taitt-Stevenson who has helped me find my "WHY" and helped me grow confidence in sharing my gift of writing. Without her loyalty and dedication to my craft, this book would not be possible.

Thank you to my literary village of warriors, my family, friends, and supporters who continue to forge forward in this crazy thing called life while inspiring my growth as a writer.

To the Divine Creator, I am sincerely thankful and grateful for the gift of words and for your divine spirit leading me where my trust and love are without borders.

Note to readers

Hello to my literary village of warriors, women, and wonderful beings,

Thank you to all who have purchased, read, gifted, shared, or donated my books. As I researched and wrote this book, I wanted you to know that I participated personally in every activity, exercise and practice suggested in this book. So, I not only talk it, I walked it. I am no judge, or dictator. I'm simply a woman dedicated to the healing journey of all that cross my path. Whether we have met personally, on social media, or only through my books, my passion and purpose remain the same. My goal is to become the best version of myself while helping you become yours. We all have had to deal with an unhealthy, toxic, unhappy, or unfulfilling relationship at some point in our lives. Those types of relationships can be very damaging to your sense of self-worth. So, it became important to me to recognize the patterns, notice the signs and break free from harmful connections and unhealthy associations. I know firsthand how tricky relationships can be. The euphoria of the right one can take you to amazing heights while the wrong one can leave your ass broken, damaged, or shattered. But there's a beautiful side to bad or unfulfilling relationships. They give us a much-needed reality check and show us what we don't want in a relationship. We learn how strong and badass we really are and how to rediscover ourselves. We can ultimately master the art of self-love and remember our worth.

Everyone could use advice or guidance from time to time and having that big sister's advice is special. It comes from a place of nonjudgment and is filled with wisdom from experiences. Big sisters will sometimes pop your hand, and rough you up a bit all in the name of love. The advice of a big sister who cares, teaches you to be mindful of your words, actions, decisions, and interactions. So, I feel that passing on my big-sister advice is the right thing to do.

After all, I really am the oldest sibling in my family. I'm here as the sister-whisperer to hold you up and walk with you as you go through whatever you're going through in your relationship, situationship or situationshit! My words may sometimes hit where it hurts, or they may feel like you got smacked with a wet bag of sand. But it's because I want you to wake up from the mindfuck. I've been a fool for love, I loved some fools and I've fooled some loves. Even the wisest woman or the wisest man can sometimes be a fool for love. That doesn't make us stupid, it makes us human! I've fallen in love too many times to count being a victim of my own optimism in the potential of my former mates. But now instead of falling, I invite you to stand up in love by standing up for yourself!

Thank you for allowing me into your space.

Sincerely,

Sonya

Forever your Big-Sister from another mister!

Introduction

After becoming the sounding board for so many of my family and friends who have been meshed into Situationships or unfulfilling, unhealthy relationships, providing support, healing and empowerment became my mission in my writing. My big sister, best friend, or auntie type of approach is nonjudgmental though a little rough at times. However, it's a tough-love approach rounded out in soft loving edges in which I've helped those closest to me reclaim themselves, emit more confidence, and make decisions that better served their own personal desires or needs. This book is filled with thought-provoking activities, humor, real talk, and empowering words to help you get through whatever you may be going through in any relationship, Situationship, or personal connection in your life.

My first book Situationships are full of Situationshit was written to bring awareness to the undefined romantic relationships that many currently refer to as Situationships. Formerly referred to as "hookups", Situationships have become more common. The term encompasses a broad array of meanings that may be unique to everyone. Nevertheless, the universal issues in Situationships can be summed up as confusion or ambiguity. Relationships that are not truly official can be subject to open interpretation. Problems can arise because people may not be on the same page or have different opinions on what constitutes a Situationship or even a good relationship.

Though we are in a world filled with electronic, communications, E-dating, E-relationships, the human nature in us still harbors a need for some sort of intimate connections. Not knowing where you stand in a relationship or not having a clear label can create gray areas of confusion. When you begin to feel undefinable and the relationship appears to have blurred lines without clear boundaries, a Situationship has likely been born. By not being someone's girlfriend, boyfriend, friend-withbenefits, significant other, fiancé, partner, or spouse, you're left in a sort of limbo. That untitled status makes the connection impalpable or even unsubstantial. So, my first book was to help bring attention to Situationships, identify what a Situationship looks like, and figure out if you were really caught up in a Situationship instead of a functional relationship.

This book, Relationships & Situationships Survival Guide, is meant to aid in handling uncomfortable relationships or Situationships. Whether you're in a relationship/Situationship, getting over one, or think you may be headed for one, this may help navigate the waters. The tools, tips, suggestions, and quotes shared in this book are meant to help you stay afloat in the area of unhealthy, unfulfilling, questionable, or stagnant relationships. No matter what path your Situationship or your relationship takes, you may find this book helpful. Whether you decide to continue in your Situationship/relationship or to finally tap out, this book can potentially help through the process.

Filled with empowering words, workable actions, tools, tips, and encouragement, the Situationships & Relationship Survival Guide can be summed up as doses of vitamin soul. Here I will provide actionable steps and advice, that will keep you engaged in the business of self-care, self-love, and self-respect.

It may help you or someone you know, stay afloat in any Situationship or challenging relationship. This book was written from experience, with an empathetic mindset because I too, have walked the walk in some draining Situationships and challenging relationships. I know firsthand how easy it is to lose yourself in relationships. More importantly, I know that reclaiming your power and finding yourself again is always possible no matter what age, what stage, or what place you are in at this moment.

Situationship Goals:
Let's not be committed,
not talk about the future,
stick parts of our bodies in each other,
not go on dates,
have sex with others,
have no accountability
and be confused on where we stand with
each other.

THE SITUATIONSHIP STARTER PACK

1. NOT LOOKING FOR A COMMITMENT

2. STAY LOYAL BUT WE AREN'T OFFICIAL

3. DON'T ACT SINGLE EVEN THOUGH WE'RE NOT TOGETHER

4. HAVE SEX, LOTS OF SEX, BUT NO SLEEPOVERS

5. ASK NO QUESTIONS, I TELL YOU NO LIES

6. DON'T CATCH FEELINGS & STAY IN YOUR LANE

7. STAY IN THE GRAY ZONE, THINGS ARE NOT BLACK AND WHITE

8. NO TITLES, NO LABELS, NO RULES ALLOWED

9. I WANT TO HOOK UP WITH YOU BUT KEEP MY OPTIONS OPEN

10. LESS TALKING MORE TEXTING TO KEEP THE VAGUE LINES OF COMMUNICATION OPEN AND CLOSED ALL AT THE SAME TIME

SIGNS OF A SITUATIONSHIP

- INCONSISTENCY AND LACK OF CLARITY
- ONE OR BOTH OF YOU ARE SEEING OTHER PEOPLE; YOU'RE NOT EXCLUSIVE BUT THERE'S JEALOUSY OR FEELINGS OF DISCOMFORT AROUND THE SUBJECT OF OTHERS IN THEIRS OR YOUR LIFE
- YOU'RE UNSURE HOW THE PERSON REALLY FEELS ABOUT YOU
- YOU DON'T KNOW WHERE YOUR STAND OR WHERE IT'S GOING; YOU HAVEN'T HAD THE DTR (DEFINE THE RELATIONSHIP) CONVERSATION
- YOUR TIME TOGETHER CONSISTS OF MOSTLY BOOTY CALLS, SEX, AND NO PLANNED DATES LIKE DINNER, MOVIES, PARTIES, ETC...
- YOU HAVEN'T MET THEIR FAMILY OR FRIENDS
- THERE'S NO DISCUSSION ABOUT THE FUTURE
- THEY ONLY MAKE LAST-MINUTE PLANS WITH YOU
- THERE'S MORE TEXTING THAN TALKING OR SPENDING TIME WITH EACH OTHER
- THE RELATIONSHIP IS NOT MOVING FORWARD

While these are just a few signs, the list is not all-inclusive. Situationships come in all shapes, sizes, and colors so the signs can vary based on your own personal interpretation.

Below are 2 links to Situationships quizzes. Take the quizzes to see where you land. You might be surprised.
https://lovely-ology.com/take-the-quiz-are-you-in-a-situationship-or-nah/
https:/www.buzzfeed.com/kellymartinez/situationship-checklist-quiz

If you are in a Situationship, you are not the other person's partner or significant other. There's probably no real romance or true intimacy (I don't mean sex). Once you start moving into the zone where you think you are owed something in the Situationship, things will get muddy. If you start going out of the way doing special things like cooking meals, washing their clothes, buying them underwear, toiletries, or intimate gifts, you've veered off into the wrong lane of a Situationship. Then if you start expecting the same special things in return, you have rolled completely off the highway down into the ditch. So, slow your roll because you should know your role. If you find yourself in the zone of unreciprocated feelings or the other person seems to want more and you don't, it's best to break things off.

Recognizing A Situationship

Situationships can be housed in the check-off-box of "It's complicated." In the beginning, it may not be complicated, but over time it can become complicated. After all, people have feelings. Emotions evolve and change. If asked if you're in a relationship and you respond, "it's complicated." That usually means, you're unsure or don't know exactly where you stand. The relationship has complexities that are contorted with anomalies making it difficult to even define your status. This is one of the many versions of a Situationship. So, you're not really single, you're kind of seeing someone, you have an intimate sexual connection but you're not exclusive or in a relationship per se. Now, what kind of fresh hell is that? Well, actually it's not really hell. You're in relationship purgatory straddling the gates between heaven and hell.
The terms aren't very clear. However, "NO" is very clear. Situationships are filled with big fat No's.

- **No Boundaries**
- **No Accountability**
- **No Rules**
- **No Commitment**
- **No Structure**

WAKING UP FROM THE IMAGINATIONSHIP OF A SITUATIONSHIP

IT'S NOT A REAL RELATIONSHIP IF:

1. You don't know where he lives and have never been to his house
2. You've known him for less than a month
3. The majority of your conversation and communication is via text
4. He wears a wedding ring but he's not married to you
5. He's dating other people and you're not
6. You don't have serious dates
7. You never talk about your relationship
8. You don't know each other's friends
9. You see them only when it's convenient for them
10. There's no talk about the future

Don't lose yourself trying to find happiness in anything or in anyone that doesn't love you back.

We can get lost in the vortex of life, love, and relationships.

Never lose yourself because you found someone. But even if you've lost yourself, you can find yourself again.

Just know that the more you find yourself and reclaim your power, the more people you will lose and that's OK.

Limiting how much of yourself you give is necessary because many have no limit on how much they take.

Being in a relationship and part of a couple doesn't mean you should lose yourself in it. While we want to make our significant other happy, it should not come at the expense of our own happiness. Neither party should be making all the decisions. You should never be giving in to all their demands. Whether it's giving in to their sexual demands, trying to get you to give up your career goals or dreams, or even isolating yourself from family and friends because of jealousy, you can get lost in the relationship if you are not careful and aware that it's happening. If your partner makes all or the majority of the decisions, there's a chance you could be losing or have already lost yourself in the relationship.

When you're losing yourself in a relationship, feelings of confusion, sadness, anger, or hostility can be a few clear red flags. Sometimes to distract yourself from the unhealthiness of the relationship, you may start engaging in behaviors such as compulsive shopping, excessive drinking, overeating, gambling, spending excessive time on social media, or even working longer hours to avoid being at home with your mate.

10 SIGNS THAT YOU COULD BE LOSING OR HAVE ALREADY LOST YOURSELF IN YOUR RELATIONSHIP

1. You're unhappy but you don't say so
2. Your dreams and goals have been pushed aside
3. You indulge in distractions to avoid conflict
4. You start losing your social life and don't go out with your friends
5. You've changed your appearance for them and not for yourself
6. You always give in to their wants, needs or demands even when you don't really want to
7. You're just going through the motions and not really feeling fulfilled
8. You no longer engage in hobbies and/or activities that you enjoyed
9. Your future revolves completely around them
10. You don't make yourself a priority and tend to the needs of your mate and/or your kids without taking much time for yourself

Defining a Good relationship

There are a lot of varying interpretations of what defines a good, committed, or real relationship. Relationships are very subjective. They look different to each individual. But regardless of the uniqueness of each person's right to define their meaning in their relationship, there is a universal element I believe is required. That element is RESPECT.

The first question people should be asking themselves is "what does a good or committed or real relationship look like to me?" It's probably a difficult question to answer because most of us have never really sat down and thought in detail about it.

I took the time one day and wrote out my definition in a ninety-nine cents composition notebook with a pink gel pen. I probably tore out the pages and balled them up at least seven or eight times before I could finally get a good handle on what a committed, real relationship meant to me. To me it had to have the following components:

Authenticity: That meant starting with my own beautiful mess and not putting on a show. Showing up from the beginning in my element, in my freedom, to be me. I was honest about my shoe obsession, my need to be meticulously organized, my phobia of insects, my love of the ocean, my disdain for stinky feet, my attraction to big, strong hands with clean fingernails, my turnoff of people who chew with their mouths open, my comfort in food, my love for cooking, my struggle to make exercise part of my daily routine, my need to be heard and speak my truth and my need to have alone time without invasion of my space. I also expect them to show up authentic and those are conversations that need to be generated from the very beginning.

A Safe Space: For me, a safe space to land and not a dangerous place to fall is necessary for my relationship. With so much drama, and craziness in the world, and our busy schedules, having someone around that makes me feel safe makes a big difference. It's not that I totally depend on my partner for everything but knowing he's my backup plan providing a cushion when things are tilted off-balance is part of my requirement.

Appreciation: Small expressions of gratitude from myself and my partner are a very necessary component. When my husband makes the bed, no matter how long we've been married (almost 23 years) I always say, "thank you babe for making the bed." Every day, he brings my favorite coffee drink and I always say thank you. He brings me flowers just because, I stick post-it notes on the mirror to remind him to take his thyroid medicine. It's the little things that go a long way.

Trust: That's a universal factor in all relationships. The foundation of any solid relationship has to be built on trust. I must trust him as he must trust me. The goal is not to own each other, but to hone each other.

Growth: No two people stay exactly the same in any relationship. Interests change, tastes change, visions change, residences change, goals change, bodies change, and health changes. And so many other things change. So, for me, my partner has to be flexible in the area of change as do I. Allowing each other space to grow is profound. So, if he notices that my roots are outgrowing the pot, he should be helping to prune me and help me replant myself, not let me stay in that pot. I also need to do the same for him.

These are the top five elements of what a healthy, committed real relationship looks like to me. While there are other additional components, I listed the top five. Your relationships should be a source of bonding, pleasure, fulfillment, and joy. It should never feel miserable, confusing, sad, or lonely.

So, the first key in surviving a Situationship or any relationship is to sit down and define what exactly a healthy relationship looks like to you.

I'm finding my joy

what does your ideal relationship look like?

WHAT IS YOUR RELATIONSHIP STATUS?

 SINGLE

 IN A RELATIONSHIP

 CRUSHING

 MARRIED

 IT'S COMPLICATED

 BROKEN HEARTED

 IN A SITUATIONSHIP!

 OTHER_____

CIRCLE THE RELATIONSHIP STATUS THAT BEST FITS WHERE YOU ARE OR WRITE YOUR STATUS ON THE "OTHER" LINE. THEN WRITE ON THE NEXT PAGE IF YOU ARE HAPPY OR UNHAPPY IN THAT STATUS AND WHY. THE PURPOSE OF THIS IS TO HELP YOU IDENTIFY WHERE YOU ARE SO THAT YOU CAN START TO CHANGE YOUR POSITION IF IT NO LONGER SERVES YOU.

My STATUS

_____

**REGARDLESS OF WHAT BOX YOU PUT YOURSELF IN,
YOUR HAPPINESS IS NOT DETERMINED BY YOUR RELATIONSHIP STATUS!
IS IT TIME TO WALK AWAY?**

sometimes people change up on you so you can master the art of letting go!

Sonyaism

Should I stay?
Should I go?
How do I know?

While there is no perfect formula to determine when it's time to walk away from a relationship, the following quiz may be helpful in ultimately making a sound decision for yourself.

On the next page read each statement and think about how it applies to your relationship

Circle T for True or F for False

Count up the number of times you answered "True"
Compare your score to the chart below to give you thoughts about the state of your relationship.

SCORE	WHAT IT ALL MEANS
40-50	AWESOME! YOU PROBABLY HAVE A KEEPER
29-39	NOT TOO BAD BUT COULD USE SOME DISCUSSION
20-28	PROBABLY A BIT TROUBLED. MAYBE CONSIDER COUNSELING IF YOUR PARTNER IS OPEN TO IT
10-19	MAY NOT BE WORTH IT. PROBABLY TIME TO WALK AWAY
0-9	THERE IS REALLY NO RELATIONSHIP. WHY ARE YOU STILL HANGING ON?

1 - I am secure in my relationship.   T or F

2 - I know where I stand in the relationship.   T or F

3 - I trust my partner.   T or F

4 - I feel I have an intimate connection with my partner.   T or F

5 - Our sex life is great.   T or F

6 - I can comfortably communicate my feelings to my partner.   T or F

7 - I don't get angry, jealous, or mad when I think about my relationship.   T or F

8 - My partner is comfortable discussing his/her problems with me.   T or F

9 - My partner and I have common goals.   T or F

10 - I can be myself around my partner.   T or F

11 - After an argument with my partner, I can cool off quickly.   T or F

12 - After an argument with me, my partner can cool off quickly.   T or F

13 - When we argue, we don't call each other names.   T or F

14 - We never fight in public or in front of our children or other people.   T or F

15 - We have date nights regularly.   T or F

16 - We like to try new things in bed.   T or F

17 - When I come home, my partner is happy to see me.   T or F

18 - When my partner comes home, I'm happy to see him/her.   T or F

19 - My partner is content/satisfied after sex.   T or F

20 - I don't discuss our relationship problems with other people.   T or F

21 - My partner doesn't discuss our relationship problems with other people.   T or F

22 - I feel like my partner has my back.   T or F

23 - We both have healthy separate lives outside of the relationship.   T or F

24 - My partner doesn't try to change me as a person.   T or F

25 - I don't try to change my partner.   T or F

26 - My partner is helpful and attentive to my needs.   T or F

27 - They have a strong sense of self and have integrity.   T or F

28 - They love all of you, even the flawed parts.   T or F

29 - They have a good sense of humor and make you laugh.   T or F

30 - They are open to compromise.   T or F

31 - They give without the expectation of anything in return.   T or F

32 - They carry themselves like a responsible adult.   T or F

33 - They admit when they are wrong and don't find apologies   T or F
difficult.

34 - They are willing to confront their inner demons and work on   T or F
healing.

35 - You both can forgive each other.   T or F

36 - They are emotionally mature and not inwardly focused.   T or F

37 - Your family likes him/her, and their family likes you.   T or F

38 - This relationship brings out the best version of me.   T or F

39 - I don't feel like I'm sacrificing more than I should for the   T or F
relationship.

40 - We laugh and have a good time more than we argue or fight.   T or F

41 - They add value to my life.   T or F

42 - I love him/her for who they are and not for who I hope them   T or F
to be.

43 - They don't blame their ex, other people, kids, or circumstances   T or F
for their life.

44 - He/she is a good listener and doesn't monopolize the   T or F
conversation.

45 - He/she makes effort to connect/ (i.e., plans dates, trips, etc....)   T or F

46 - He/she is reliable and keeps their word.   T or F

47 - He/she is responsible with money.   T or F

48 - He/she appears to accept constructive criticism and accept   T or F
feedback, then take responsibility and be willing to self-reflect
and work towards improvement.

49 - I don't feel anxious, depressed or confused in my relationship.   T or F

50 - You genuinely like your partner.   T or F

Now that you've answered the questions,
ask yourself if staying in the
Situationship or relationship is truly
a healthy choice for
both of you.

Maybe you need to rethink your Dream Girls "I'm
Stayin, I'm Stayin and you and you and you, you're
gonna love me" mindset!

AM I ADEQUATELY MEETING MY OWN NEEDS OR
AM I EXPECTING MY PARTNER TO MEET THEM?

NEEDS YOUR PARTNER SHOULD NOT
BE EXPECTED TO MEET

1. IMPROVEMENT OF YOUR SELF-ESTEEM
2. BOOSTING YOUR SELF-CONFIDENCE
3. STRENGTHENING YOUR SELF-ACCEPTANCE
4. BUILDING STRONGER SELF-LOVE
5. HEALING YOUR PERSONAL PAST TRAUMA
6. CARRYING YOUR PERSONAL BAGGAGE THAT YOU BROUGHT
TO THE RELATIONSHIP
7. TO BE YOUR EVERYTHING
8. TO ALWAYS EMPATHIZE WITH YOU AND UNDERSTAND WHAT
YOU'RE GOING THROUGH

THINGS YOU SHOULD EXPECT FROM YOUR PARTNER

1. RESPECT
2. LOYALTY
3. AFFECTION
4. COMPASSION
5. EMPATHY
6. TIME
7. ATTENTION
8. KINDNESS AND GENEROSITY
9. TRUST

Relationship Do's and Don'ts

DO THIS

- Do have realistic expectations
- Do pick your battles wisely
- Do give each other space
- Do keep yourself grounded
- Do be forgiving
- Do keep doing things that you enjoy without them
- Do keep your own friendships and connections
- Do your best to be empathetic
- Do be patient and loving
- Do be supportive
- Do take time to learn each other's love language
- Do talk things out
- Do apologize when you're in the wrong

NOT THIS

- Don't make them choose between you and their children
- Don't make them choose between you and their mom
- Don't expect them to never notice another woman/man
- Don't push them to give up their passion, hobbies, or purpose
- Don't make them give up their friends for you
- Don't expect them to be a different person
- Don't expect them to spend all their free time with you
- Don't expect them to always apologize first
- Don't expect them to have no friends of the gender they are attracted to
- Don't expect them to fulfill the voids in your life
- Don't expect your partner to read your mind
- Don't rely on them to make you happy
- Don't compare your relationship to anyone else's
- Don't put other people in your business
- Don't hold grudges or keep score

SOME OF YOU ARE
CONFUSING CHAOS
WITH CHEMISTRY.
YOU HAVE TO BE
BRAVE ENOUGH TO
SAY, "THIS IS NO
LONGER WHAT I WANT"
AND MOVE OUT OF THE
CHAOS AND INTO
SOME CALM.
SOMETIMES YOU
SIMPLY HAVE TO MAKE
A DECISION THAT
HURTS YOUR HEART
BUT HEALS YOUR SOUL.

Do I stay or do I go?

What are the benefits of staying?

What would be the advantages of going?

Strong women wear their pain, their challenges and their hurt like they wear their stilettos.
No matter how much it hurts, you never see the pain, you only see the beauty and grace of it.

WHAT CHALLENGES, RESPONSIBILITIES OR STRUGGLES ARE YOU WALKING IN WITH GRACE AND STRENGTH?
WRITE THEM ON, AROUND OR NEXT TO EACH SHOE.

WHAT ACTIONS CAN YOU TAKE TO MAKE THOSE CHALLENGES IN THOSE HEELS MORE COMFORTABLE OR BEARABLE?
WRITE THEM ON, AROUND OR NEXT TO EACH SLIPPER.

The new and improved you

LIST 3 WAYS YOU HAVE GROWN AS A PERSON IN THE PAST YEAR

LIST 3 THINGS ABOUT YOURSELF THAT HAVE IMPROVED AND CHANGED FOR THE BETTER IN THE PAST YEAR

7 TIPS FOR IMPROVING YOUR VERSION

1. Know that your best version of yourself is your own vision and no one else's version or expectation

2. Aim to be present, not perfect

3. Remember what you do (your job, raising families, supporting partners, being a dedicated mom or loyal friend, etc.) is not who you are; these things are what you do. Who you truly are and what you do are not the same so spend more time nurturing the WHO. It's not selfish, it's self-care

4. Learn one new thing each month (a new word, hobby, language, activity, etc.)

5. Once a month treat yourself to some type of personal care (facial, spa, mani-pedi, massage, etc.)

6. Work on your spirituality and strengthen your spiritual ground. Whether it's meditation, prayer, yoga, going to a place of worship, or connecting with a group of spiritually-minded people, spirituality is essential to self-improvement

7. Be adventurous, take chances and step outside of your usual self

YOUR GLOW IS SO MAGICAL AND BRIGHT WHEN NO ONE'S GOOFY, DUSTY ASS SON IS STRESSING YOU THE F... OUT! GLOW AND SHINE SO DAMN BRIGHTLY THAT IT HURTS THEIR F---ING EYES!!!

Sonyaism

29

GET YOUR GLOW ON & EMBRACE YOUR INNER UNICORN

ADD SOME GLITTER TO YOUR LIFE TODAY
EVEN IF IT'S NOT YOUR THING, JUST FOR TODAY TRY ONE OF THESE
SPARKLE MOMENTS

1. PUT ON AN ARTICLE OF SEQUINED CLOTHING
2. WEAR GLITTER EYESHADOW
3. WEAR SPARKLE LIPSTICK
4. POLISH YOUR NAILS WITH GLITTER POLISH
5. PUT SOME BODY BRONZER OR FENTY DIAMOND BOMB ON
   YOUR NECK AND CHEST. IF YOU'RE BOLD ENOUGH PUT IT ON
   YOUR FACE TOO!

DON'T BE AFRAID TO SPARKLE
LIGHT UP THE WHOLE DAMN ROOM!

SHINE BRIGHT LIKE A DIAMOND

DON'T BE A WOMAN BUILDING UP A MAN FOR THE NEXT WOMAN, WHILE HE'S WREAKING HAVOC AND DAMAGING YOU FOR THE NEXT MAN.

Sonyaism

ARE YOU TAKING BRICKS FROM YOUR PAST RELATIONSHIP INTO YOUR NEW ONE?

IF YOU HAUL THOSE BRICKS FROM YOUR LAST RELATIONSHIP INTO YOUR NEW ONE, YOU'LL CREATE THE SAME BUILDING THAT BROKE UNDER PRESSURE

FEAR, IMPATIENCE, MISTRUST, CONTROL ISSUES, LOW SELF-ESTEEM, DADDY ISSUES, MOMMY ISSUES, DOUBT, BITTERNESS, CODEPENDENCY, PAIN, ANGER, JEALOUSY

TRY STARTING WITH NEW BRICKS SUCH AS...

SELF-CONTROL, PATIENCE, SELFCARE, SELF-RESPECT, BOUNDARIES, GROWTH, FORGIVENESS, SUPPORT, HAPPINESS WITH YOURSELF, GOALS, PASSION, SPIRITUAL GROUNDING

START WITH NEW BRICKS!!!
WRITE ON THE BRICKS BELOW THOUGHTS AND BEHAVIOR PATTERNS YOU ARE BRINGING OR WANT TO BRING INTO BUILDING YOUR NEW RELATIONSHIP

save up to

70%

shop now

You are not bargain-basement material!!! Take yourself off the clearance rack and position yourself in the locked case behind the locked glass where all of the valuables are stored! You are too high-end for bargain shopper relationships!

flash sale

LIST 10 THINGS PERSONALLY ABOUT YOURSELF THAT MAKES YOU EVEN MORE VALUABLE

I am...

Closure is overrated

closure is overrated. there will come a time when you will have to decide to keep turning the pages and jumping to the next chapter or simply closing the book. most times the only closure you need is peace of mind and simply knowing that you deserve better.

sonyaism

WRITE THE THINGS YOU NEED TO CLOSE IN THE BOOK BELOW

Self-Care
PRACTICES

- ♥ Create A Morning Routine
- ♥ Eat Something Healthy
- ♥ Drink Lots Of Water
- ♥ Try Yoga Or Pilates
- ♥ Meditate for 5 minutes
- ♥ Listen To An Inspiring Podcast
- ♥ Write Down What You're Grateful For
- ♥ Put On Happy Music & Just Listen

Of the infinite number of ways we bully one another into second-guessing what we should or shouldn't be doing with our lives and relationships, coming in at the top of the list is the classic "you can do better than him/her". It always perplexes me when I hear that or hear "she or he can do better". I'm always confused by how family and/or friends always feel it is necessary and ok to approve or disapprove of someone's relationship. What I've found is most often people may believe they're looking out for your best interests, but in actuality, it's their own ego's way of just trying to make themselves feel better by judging you. That's why you should keep relationship business to yourself!

KEEP YOUR RELATIONSHIP BUSINESS PRIVATE

STOP ASKING FRIENDS AND FAMILY FOR RELATIONSHIP ADVICE

TRUST YOUR OWN INSTINCTS, INTUITION, AND INNER VOICE !

KEEP RELATIONSHIP PROBLEMS, DISCUSSIONS LIMITED TO:

YOUR THERAPIST
YOUR JOURNAL
YOURSELF
GOD
OR 1 PERSON YOU TRUST COMPLETELY, THAT WOULD NOT JUDGE YOU AND YOU ARE
CONFIDENT HAS YOUR BEST INTEREST AT HEART

You can be
marriage material
mate material or
mattress material.

If you are material that
matters, valuable and
worth the investment,
don't allow yourself to
be treated like cheap
ass corduroy when you
know you are Vicuna
Wool!
$3000.00 per yard
Vicuna Wool
$8.00 per yard
corduroy
The fabric of your being
is valuable!

MARRIAGE OR MATE MATERIAL

- **EMOTIONALLY AVAILABLE**
- **RELIABLE**
- **SELF-SUFFICIENT**
- **YOU CAN BE YOURSELF WITH THEM**
- **THEY PAY ATTENTION TO THE SMALL THINGS**
- **YOU HAVE SIMILAR GOALS AND ARE HEADED IN THE SAME DIRECTION**
- **YOUR CORE VALUES ARE IN ALIGNMENT**
- **THEY HAVE A HEALTHY SENSE OF HUMOR**
- **YOU CAN HAVE INTIMACY WITHOUT SEX**
- **YOU ARE COMPATIBLE SEXUALLY BUT IT'S NOT ALL ABOUT SEX IN YOUR RELATIONSHIP**

MATTRESS MATERIAL

- LACK OF COMMUNICATION
- BOOTY CALLS/MOST INTERACTION INVOLVES ONLY SEX
- MOST COMMUNICATION IS VIA TEXT OR MESSAGING
- LAZY
- HAS NO GOALS
- SPENDS MOST OF THEIR TIME IN THE VIRTUAL WORLD INSTEAD OF THE REAL WORLD
- ALREADY MARRIED, IN A RELATIONSHIP OR LIVES WITH SOMEONE
- STANDS YOU UP OR ISN'T INTERESTED IN GOING OUT ON DATES WITH YOU
- POOR EFFORT

IF YOUR RELATIONSHIP STARTED BY PRESSING "LIKE" ON A POST OR PIC AND FIFTY PERCENT OR MORE OF YOUR CONVERSATION IS VIA TEXT, YOU ARE NOT IN A RELATIONSHIP...
YOU ARE IN A TEXTATIONSHIP!

WHILE NO QUIZ CAN GIVE YOU DEFINITIVE ANSWERS, THE QUESTIONS BELOW CAN POSSIBLY HELP YOU ANALYZE THE SITUATION AND DETERMINE IF YOU'RE IN A TEXTATIONSHIP OR PSEUDO-RELATIONSHIP.

Check off the applicable boxes. If you check off more than 3 of those boxes, you're probably in a pseudo-relationship or Textationship.

- [ ] They are always busy
- [ ] You communicate mostly or always via text
- [ ] Overall, you are confused about this relationship
- [ ] You feel you can't trust them or they are hiding something
- [ ] You have mostly E-communication (i.e., social media, text, email)
- [ ] You do more sexting than having actual sex
- [ ] You rarely or never go on dates
- [ ] You rarely or never see them in person
- [ ] They leave you on "read" without responding to your text
- [ ] You feel taken and lonely at the same time
- [ ] They never make plans with you
- [ ] You wonder if they are involved with someone else
- [ ] You rarely have meaningful discussions
- [ ] There's no talk of the future
- [ ] You've never met face-to-face

HOW MANY TEXTS DID YOU GET FROM THEM TODAY?

HOW MANY TEXTS DID YOU GET WITHOUT YOU HAVING TO TEXT FIRST?

HOW MANY FACE-TO-FACE CONVERSATIONS HAVE YOU HAD IN THE PAST 30 DAYS?

HOW MANY TIMES HAVE YOU GONE OUT TOGETHER IN THE PAST 30 DAYS?

ASK YOURSELF:
IS THIS ENOUGH FOR ME?
DO I WANT & NEED MORE?

IT MAY BE TIME FOR THE TEXATIONSHIP TAPOUT OR THE PSEUDO-RELATIONSHIP SAYONARA!

NOW WHAT?

SCHEDULE A DATE, A LOW-MAINTENANCE DATE LIKE BREAKFAST, COFFEE, LUNCH, OR A PICNIC. GIVE THEM TWO OR THREE CHANCES. IF THEY CANCEL, MAKE EXCUSES, OR DON'T SHOW UP, THAT'S A RED FLAG ALERT!

They are not just that into you and that's OK. Move on.

PEOPLE WHO MAKE TIME MATTER AND PEOPLE WHO MATTER MAKE TIME.

IF YOU'RE TIRED OF DEALING WITH JOKERS AND CLOWNS, WHY DO YOU KEEP GOING TO THE CIRCUS, SEEKING SIMPLE ENTERTAINMENT?

PUTTING YOUR IMAGINARY CROWN ON A JOKER OR A CLOWN STILL WON'T MAKE HIM A KING!

COLOR BY NUMBERS
CLOWN OR NAH?

1—Red   3—Blue   5—Orange   7—Brown
2—Yellow   4—Green   6—Purple   8—Black

1. Color Red if he's married, lives with another woman or cheats
2. Color Yellow if he doesn't keep promises or stands you up
3. Color blue if your family or friends don't like him
4. Color Green if you don't spend quality time together or most of your time together is for booty calls
5. Color Orange if he never makes plans with you or if you're the only one planning dates and time together
6. Color Purple if he brings out the crazy in you
7. Color Brown if he never wants to talk about the future or make it clear where you stand in his life
8. Color Black if you find yourself feeling drained, sad or angry more than happy and fulfilled

MOVING ON! NO REGRETS!

Hey, are my calls and messages coming through?

10:00

Oh no, I did see your message and saw your missed call but when the world stopped revolving around you, I was too busy doing me to respond!

10:02

~Sonyaism~

THAT FUNNY MOMENT WHEN YOU IMAGINE THEIR FACE AFTER THEY TRY TO SLIDE UP IN YOUR DM AND YOU DON'T REPLY BUT KEEP COMMENTING ON THEIR TIMELINE TO EVERYONE ELSE!!! LOL YEAH... I SEE YOU MOFO, BUT I'M NOT BEAT.

SHUTTING A FUCK BOY DOWN
(real text exchange word for word)
He IM's her after a year when he disrespected her and played her for another woman

Him: Hi, I never got a chance to apologize to you. It wasn't supposed to happen that way. I was being childish and a coward. I could've handled things differently. I just want you to know I'm truly sorry for the way I acted. U may never forgive me.
Her: I forgave you a long time ago J… You've experienced my energy already so you know who and what I am
Him: DAMN! U still fine as hell!!!
Her: Duhhhhh
Him: do I gotta get on my hands & knees?
Her: For??????????
Him: to regain your trust
Her: regain me and my trust? Speak a little more clearly on what you're trying to ask me
Him: I wanna reintroduce myself
Her: why would you need to do that?
Him: I felt like I handled things like a little boy and I wanted to give you the grown man version of myself. I'm on my knees asking for a second chance
Her: if you need a friend I'm here. That's who I am and that's who you lost out on. But you and I will never be more than that. Real men don't need to kneel down and beg unless you're kneeling to propose. So keep standing. Regardless of how fucked up you treated me, you're still a KING… so just believe in that and be better for the next woman. Deuces
Her: ✌️
Him: no response
I imagine crickets in the background LOL!!!
Now that is how you shut a FUCKBOY DOWN!!!!

IF THEIR PRESENCE ADDS NO
VALUE TO YOUR LIFE
THEIR ABSENCE WILL MAKE
NO DIFFERENCE
YOU CAN'T CHANGE ANOTHER
PERSON, BUT YOU CAN
ALWAYS CHANGE DIRECTIONS

"

SOMETIMES YOU HAVE TO FORGET WHAT YOU FEEL AND BURY WHAT YOU HOPED FOR TO REMEMBER WHAT YOU DESERVE!

SONYAISM

Adding value to your life

LIST 10 THINGS ABOUT YOUR MATE, SIGNIFICANT OTHER, PARTNER THAT ADDS VALUE TO YOUR LIFE

Adding value to your life

LIST 10 THINGS YOU DESERVE AND ARE GETTING FROM
YOUR RELATIONSHIP

_____

_____

_____

_____

_____

_____

_____

_____

_____

_____

_____

_____

_____

_____

_____

_____

_____

**IF YOU ARE HAVING A HARD TIME LISTING 10
THINGS, ASK YOURSELF, IS THERE REALLY
VALUE IN THIS FOR ME?**

WOMEN I KNOW...
4 HOURS AFTER A BREAKUP
WILL HAVE
2 HIGH PAYING JOBS,
A NEW BUSINESS VENTURE,
DOWN PAYMENT ON A HOUSE
AND TEST DRIVING AN X6

OLD BOY WILL STILL BE BRINGING HIS CONTRACTOR
BAGS FULL OF CLOTHES AND UNMATCHING SOCKS TO
HIS NEW CHICK'S HOUSE FALLING IN LOVE QUICK
CAUSE HE NEEDS A NEW PLACE TO STAY!!!
LOL
THE DIFFERENCE BETWEEN BOSSED UP & TOSSED UP!

Sometimes the break-up is the shake up for you to wake up from the mind f--k!

SONYAISM

HOW TO BOSS UP AFTER A BREAKUP

Create your own empowering self-care playlist
It can be songs that make you feel mellow or songs that make you
want to pump up the volume and sing out loud.
To spark inspiration and create a starting point to help you create
your own personal power playlist.
Some suggestions are listed below.

Songs give you goosebumps or butterflies
Songs that make you want to dance
Songs that make you smile
Songs that make you feel like you can kick ass
Songs you can't get out of your head
Songs that remind you that you are worthy
Songs that remind you that you are beautiful
Songs that make you snot-nose ugly cry
Songs that bring out the bold, beautiful, badass, or bitch in you
Songs that make you feel calm or relaxed

You can create more than one playlist of course and listen to what is
in alignment with your needs and mood at that moment. Think about
your reasons for that playlist then expand it out on that feeling.
Music has always been one of my favorite self-care tools. So I have
several playlists. Some of my playlists are titled as follows:

"Middle fingers up breakup"
"Soul Fuel"
"All up in my Zen"
"My Brave is Beautiful"

So create your lists grab your airpods or headphones and get into
your own zone!

How to boss up after a break-up

AFTER YOUR LAST BREAK-UP, LIST THE WAYS YOU BOSSED UP!

HAVING A GOOD HEART AND BEING A LOVING GIVING PERSON ARE BEAUTIFUL QUALITIES; BUT AS GOOD AS YOU ARE, YOU DON'T ALWAYS HAVE TO FEED PEOPLE FROM YOUR SOUL BECAUSE THERE ARE A LOT OF PEOPLE WHO ONLY DESERVE A DOGGY BAG OR A PAPER PLATE TO GO!

sonyaism

HOW TO STOP GIVING TOO MUCH IN YOUR RELATIONSHIP

- PRIORITIZE YOURSELF & PUT YOUR NEEDS FIRST
- START BEING MINDFUL OF HOW OFTEN YOU SAY YES, WHY YOU'RE SAYING YES, AND WHAT YOU'RE SAYING YES TO
- THINK WITH YOUR HEAD, NOT WITH YOUR HEART
- KEEP YOURSELF BUSY
- SAY NO MORE OFTEN (EVEN IF IT'S IN A SOFT/NICE WAY)
- IDENTIFY THE TAKERS OR USERS IN YOUR LIFE
- CUT OFF HABITUAL BORROWERS AND THOSE WHO DON'T KEEP THEIR WORD
- KEEP TRACK OF HOW OFTEN YOU ARE GIVING
- STOP POURING FROM AN EMPTY CUP

REMEMBER YOU OWE NO PARTS OF YOURSELF TO ANYONE.

PUT YOURSELF FIRST!

IT'S OK NOT TO RESPOND TO A TEXT, DM, OR ANSWER THAT PHONE CALL!

Sonyaism

Don't allow yourself to be a multiple choice option.
Even being "number one" makes you a multiple choice option.
Being the ONLY one should be the ONLY OPTION!
You don't belong in anyone's check off box of options!

STOP PLAYING THE OPTION POSITION

RECOGNIZE THE USERS IN YOUR LIFE, EVEN FAMILY OR FRIENDS.

PUT UP A POST-IT NOTE OR PIN A LIST OF YOUR VALUABLE ASSETS SOMEWHERE SO THAT YOU CAN SEE IT EVERY DAY TO REMIND YOU THAT YOU BELONG IN NO ONE'S CHECK-OFF BOX OF OPTIONS.

IF YOU ARE READY TO STEP OUTSIDE OF THIS CHECKOFF BOX OF OPTIONS, TRY THIS SCRIPT OR WRITE YOUR OWN:

"HEY _____.
I WANT TO SAY FIRST I LIKE YOU AND CARE ABOUT YOU, AND I THOUGHT I WAS FEELING SOMETHING SPECIAL HAPPENING BETWEEN US. BUT I NEED MORE EFFORT ON YOUR PART IF WE ARE GOING TO CONTINUE SEEING EACH OTHER. IF I'M NOT THE ONE AND THIS VIBE BETWEEN US ISN'T GOOD FOR YOU, I UNDERSTAND. PEOPLE'S NEEDS AND DESIRES CHANGE REGULARLY.
JUST MAN UP AND SAY YOU'RE JUST NOT INTO ME. I'M STRONG AND HAPPY ENOUGH IN MYSELF TO HANDLE ANY TRUTH. SO, LET'S KEEP IT REAL.
.

NEVER BE ANYONE'S SPARETIME, PASTIME, SICKTIME, MEANTIME, SOMETIME, OR PART-TIME! IF THEY AREN'T PUTTING IN OVERTIME FOR YOUR PEACETIME FOR A LIFETIME... IT'S A WASTE OF TIME!

SONYAISM

Your time is valuable

How long have you been in your relationship or situationship?

Is it still serving your needs & meeting your expectations?

How much more time are you willing to invest?

KNOW THE DIFFERENCE BETWEEN PATIENCE AND WASTING YOUR TIME!

If they sorta treat you like a girlfriend, f--ks you like a girlfriend, expects you to be supportive like a girlfriend, but hasn't really given you the commitment of such and not acknowledged you with a title...
They are using the gray area of "Not sure where we stand" as a loophole so they can bounce and move on whenever they want!
You are not a placeholder,
You are a constant!

sonyaism

10 SIGNS OF BEING A PLACEHOLDER

- *YOU WERE A REBOUND*
- *THEY RARELY OR NEVER PUT YOUR FIRST. YOU'RE OFTEN AN AFTERTHOUGHT*
- *THEY NEVER MAKE PLANS OR DATES AND YOU HAVE TO INITIATE EVERYTHING*
- *THERE ARE NO SERIOUS LIFE DISCUSSIONS*
- *THERE ARE NO PICS OF THE TWO OF YOU TOGETHER ON SOCIAL MEDIA*
- *YOU OFTEN FEEL LEFT OUT, NOT INCLUDED IN THEIR LIFE*
- *THEY OFTEN ATTEND FUNCTIONS WITHOUT YOU*
- *YOU NEVER MET THEIR FAMILY OR CLOSE FRIENDS*
- *THEY HAVE PROFILES ON DATING APPS*
- *THEY ARE NOT REALLY INTERESTED IN YOUR LIFE, LIKES, OR GOALS*

yes

no

maybe so

THE UNIVERSE
HAS ALREADY
VALIDATED
YOU, YOUR
JOURNEY,
AND YOUR
PURPOSE, SO
YOU DON'T
NEED
VALIDATION
FROM
ANYONE
ELSE!

5 WAYS

to strengthen your validity

Stop your inner critic & drown out the mean voice in your head

Write a love note to yourself

Write down three daily accomplishments or tasks you completed

Turn Off Social Media for a day or two or even more

List one skill that you have that you feel you are exceptionally good at

Sometimes in the search of a mate, you can wind up with a project instead of a partner! It's not your job to heal another's hurt or let them bleed on you from their emotional cutting and past trauma. You are not a rehabilitation center for someone else's broken pieces. It's ok to tap out and move on without feeling guilty!

NO is a complete sentence all by itself!

SIGNS OF A FIXER-UPPER MATE

(RED FLAGS)

- They always make excuses 🚩
- Blames his past or others and doesn't take responsibility 🚩
- You are constantly playing teacher or instructing him on what he should be doing or how he should be treating you 🚩
- He's a mama's boy or grandma's boy 🚩
- Never lived on his own 🚩
- Multiple children with multiple women 🚩
- Drug or alcohol abuse or addiction 🚩
- It feels like a project 🚩
- You pay all or most of the bills 🚩
- Frequent arguments about his choices or behavior 🚩
- The number of times they disappoint you outweighs the number of times they come through 🚩
- You take multiple relationship breaks 🚩
- They can't take constructive criticism 🚩
- You communicate your feelings and concerns, but nothing seems to change 🚩
- He often uses the words "I'm trying" but is never really DOING or taking action to make things happen 🚩

CIRCLE THE FLAGS ABOVE. IF YOU CIRCLED 3 OR MORE FLAGS, HE'S MORE PROJECT MATERIAL THAN PARTNER MATERIAL.
THE PACKAGE MAY LOOK GREAT ON THE OUTSIDE, BUT DAMAGED OR FRAGILE ON THE INSIDE.
SO, EITHER TAP OUT OR ACCEPT THE PROJECT AND GET TO WORK!

It doesn't matter if it's a relative, lover, romantic interest, new friend, old friend, colleague, etc. people often have to be assessed to see if they are in alignment with your well-being. You often have to reposition people in your living space for
peace of mind.
Remember it's ok to love people from a safe distance in order to protect your heart, calm your mind, settle your spirit and
enlighten your soul!

sonyaism

Distanced Loved

LIST THINGS, BEHAVIORS, ACTIVITIES, OR PEOPLE THAT ARE
FRUSTRATING YOU, AGGRAVATING YOUR SPIRIT, OR MAKING
YOU FEEL UNSETTLED.

Note to Self

Stop responding
Delete
Block
Ignore
Say no

Sonyaism

NOTICE

HEALING IS A JOURNEY OF EXPLORATION ALONG A ROAD UNDER CONSTRUCTION THAT WILL LEAD BACK TO YOUR ESSENTIAL SELF! NOW THE ROAD WILL NOT BE SMOOTHLY PAVED AND THERE MAY BE MANY DETOURS BUT STAY ON THE PATH!!! NO MATTER HOW ROUGH THAT ROAD IS, ALWAYS REMEMBER THE DESTINATION IS YOU!!!

YOU ARE WORTH THE TRIP!

Sonyaism

LETTING GO FOR HEALING

WRITE IN THE BALLOONS, THOUGHTS, HABITS,
OR BEHAVIORS THAT YOU ARE HOLDING ONTO
THAT ARE NO LONGER SERVING YOU. IMAGINE
EACH BALLOON FLOATING AWAY.

Following your heart
and being in love
takes a lot of energy.
Some fall in love
quickly. But instead
of falling in love, try
standing up in love.
There's nothing wrong
with following your
heart... just make sure
you take your brain
along on the trip!

Sonyaism

TRUST
YOURSELF

Be very selective about who is allowed access in your mental, physical and emotional space! Energy vampires and spirit leeches are everywhere. You aren't crazy, that uncomfortable vibration is your mind's way of warning you around unsafe people!
Trust your instinct!

Sonyaism

STRENGTHENING YOUR INTUITION & INSTINCTS

- **DEEPEN YOUR INTUITION THROUGH MEDITATION:** MEDITATION STRENGTHENS AND TUNES UP EVERY PART OF YOUR BODY AND MIND. IF YOU DON'T PRACTICE MEDITATION, IT'S EASY TO LEARN. IN AS LITTLE AS 10 MINUTES PER DAY, YOU CAN MASTER MINDFUL MEDITATION. THIS WILL HELP STRENGTHEN YOUR INTUITION.

- **RECOGNIZE YOUR VOICE OF INTUITION & INSTINCT:** IT'S VERY SUBTLE SO IT MAY NOT BE NOTICEABLE UNTIL YOU LEARN TO TUNE IN. IT COMMUNICATES IN VARIOUS WAYS DEPENDING ON THE PERSON. SOMETIMES IT'S SIMPLY A HUNCH, BUTTERFLIES IN YOUR STOMACH, UNEASINESS AROUND CERTAIN PEOPLE OR PLACES, GOOSEBUMPS, OR EVEN A FUNNY TASTE IN YOUR MOUTH. SO, TAKE NOTICE OF HOW YOUR BODY RESPONDS TO PEOPLE, SITUATIONS, OR PLACES.

- **PRACTICE SENSING PEOPLE BEFORE REALLY GETTING TO KNOW THEM:** DON'T RELY ON OTHERS' OPINIONS ABOUT THE PERSON. KNOW THAT PEOPLE'S ENERGY INTRODUCES THEM BEFORE THEY EVEN SPEAK. WATCH HOW THEY MOVE, LOOK AT THEIR EYES, AND SEE IF YOUR GUT FEELS UNCOMFORTABLE. DO YOU FEEL OFF OR RELAXED? DO YOU FEEL CALM OR SENSE SOME ANXIETY?

- **DO SOME BREATHWORK EXERCISES:** CONSCIOUS BREATHING PRACTICES ARE BENEFICIAL TO ALL ASPECTS OF YOUR LIFE. THERE'S A SIMPLE BREATHING METHOD CALLED THE 4-7-8 TECHNIQUE WHICH IS SHARED ON THE NEXT PAGE.

FIRST, GET INTO A COMFORTABLE SITTING POSITION. THEN PUT THE TIP OF YOUR TONGUE ON THE TISSUE RIGHT BEHIND THE TOP FRONT TEETH AND FOCUS ON THE FOLLOWING BREATHING PATTERN

- EMPTY THE LUNGS OF AIR
- BREATHE IN QUIETLY THROUGH THE NOSE FOR 4 SECONDS
- HOLD THE BREATH FOR A COUNT OF 7 SECONDS
- EXHALE FORCEFULLY THROUGH THE MOUTH, PURSING THE LIPS AND MAKING A "WHOOSH" SOUND, FOR 8 SECONDS
- REPEAT THE CYCLE UP TO 4 TIMES

PAY ATTENTION TO FEELINGS OF CONFUSION, DISCOMFORT, OR UNEASINESS IN YOUR SURROUNDINGS. NOTICE WHERE YOU ARE, WHO'S AROUND, AND WHAT IS HAPPENING. YOUR INTUITION AND INSTINCT WILL OFTEN STEER YOU AWAY FROM SOMETHING THAT ISN'T HEALTHY FOR YOU OR DOESN'T SERVE YOU. LIKEWISE, IF THE FEELING OF PEACE OR COMFORTABILITY COMES OVER YOU, YOUR INTUITION IS GUIDING YOU DOWN A PATH TO SOMETHING MORE IN ALIGNMENT WITH YOUR JOURNEY.

REFERENCE: HTTPS://WWW.VERYWELLMIND.COM/WHAT-IS-4-7-8-BREATHING -5204438

U P G R A D E

Don't let a failed
relationship make you
question yourself or
lower your standards.
Maybe it failed to make
you elevate your
standards because it was
time for you to upgrade!!!

THE UPGRADE

Now that they're gone,
what positive things have
you noticed?

What things are you more
conscious or aware of?

How are you upgrading?

NEVER CHASE HARD TO CARRY, HARD TO GET OR HARD TO READ LOVE.

Sonyaism

How to stop
THE CHASE

1 Practice self-love, self-respect, and do a self-check. Decide on something you will do daily solely for yourself. Some examples might be to read a positive quote or affirmation, write yourself a love note or mantra on a post-it and tape it to your mirror then say it out loud each morning.

2 Remember to chase your dreams, your passion, your purpose and not people.

3 Stop focusing on being lonely and stop counting your single days.

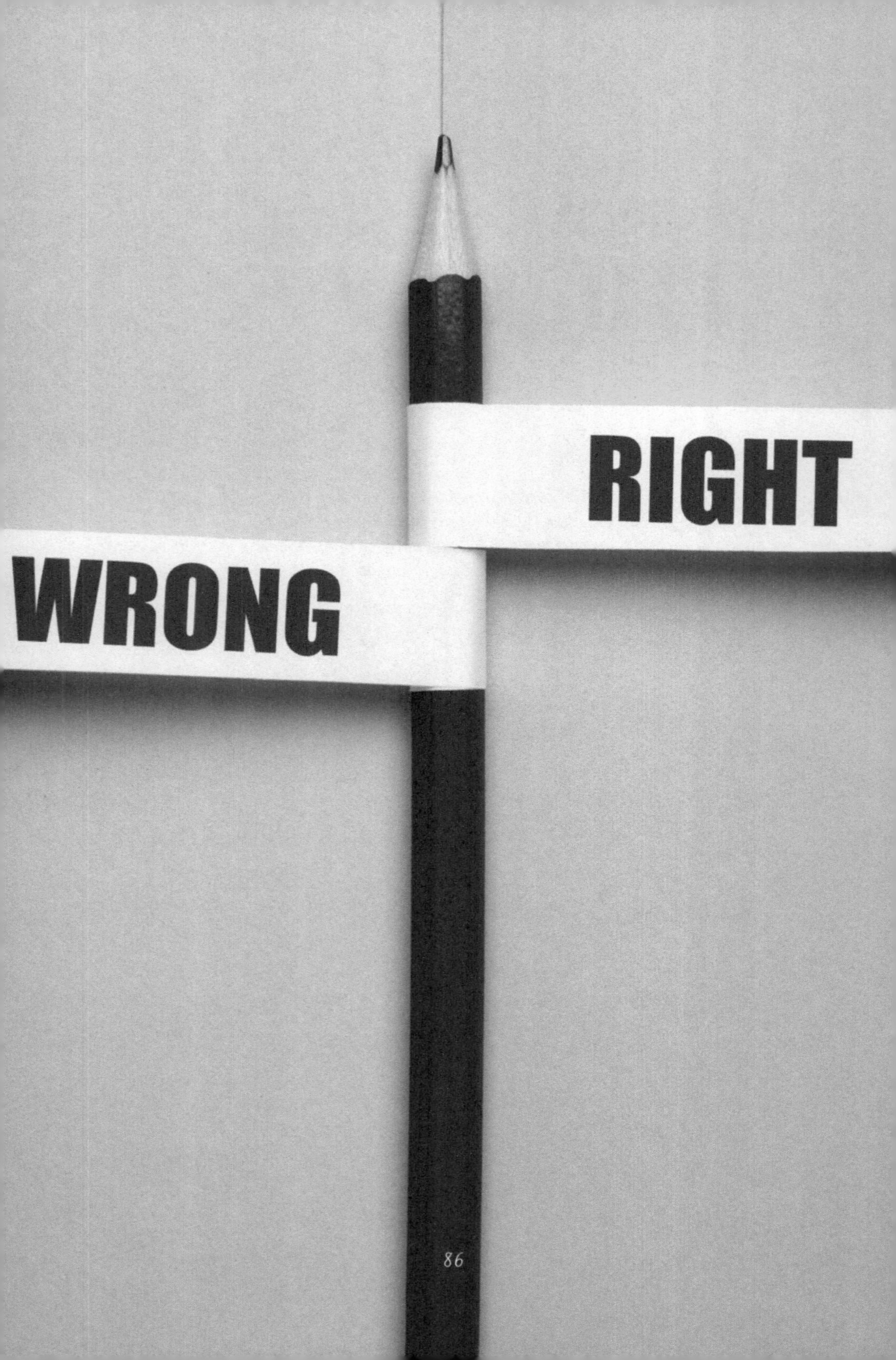
RIGHT
WRONG

"It's important
to recognize
the subtle
differences
between
Mr. Right,
Mr. Wrong
and
Mr. Right Now"

Sonyaism

How to know the difference between Mr. Right, Mr. Right Now, and Mr. Wrong, depends on each person and where you are mentally and emotionally. However, I put together a table below as a guide. Feel free to modify it and tweak it to your own specifications.

	MR. RIGHT	MR. RIGHT NOW	MR. WRONG
COMMUNICATION	YOU CAN TALK ABOUT ANYTHING COMFORTABLY AND OPENLY. CONVERSATIONS ARE INTERESTING AND HAVE SOME INTELLECTUAL COMPONENTS	CONVERSATIONS ARE NOT TOO DEEP. HE SEEMS SOMEWHAT INTERESTED BUT NOT REALLY INTELLECTUAL AND HE CAN SEEM DISINTERESTED OR BORED. YOU CAN ALSO FIND HIS CONVERSATION BORING OR NOT INTERESTING	NO CONVERSATIONS ABOUT ANYTHING MEANINGFUL. NOT INTERESTED IN WHAT YOU HAVE TO SAY. RARELY LOOKS YOU IN THE EYE OR HEARS WHAT YOU SAY
COMPATABILITY	YOU HAVE A LOT IN COMMON. YOU LIKE TRYING NEW THINGS TOGETHER. HE'S INTERESTED IN EXPLORING THINGS YOU LIKE TO DO. YOU GET ALONG VERY WELL	SHOWS SOME INTEREST IN THINGS YOU ENJOY BUT ISN'T VERY FLEXIBLE IN TRYING NEW THINGS WITH YOU. YOU DON'T HAVE MUCH IN COMMON	NOT INTERESTED IN ANYTHING YOU ENJOY. UNWILLING TO TRY NEW THINGS WITH YOU. IT'S ALL ABOUT HIM. YOU HAVE NOTHING IN COMMON
SEX	GREAT SEXUAL CHEMISTRY BUT YOU KNOW THE RELATIONSHIP COULD STILL BE FULFILLING EVEN WITHOUT IT	SEX CAN BE GREAT BUT YOU FEEL THE RELATIONSHIP WITHOUT IT WOULD BE UNFULFILLING	IT'S ALL ABOUT SEX. IF HE DOESN'T GET HIS WAY SEXUALLY IT CAN BECOME A PROBLEM. YOU'RE A BOOTY CALL. LEAVES RIGHT AFTER SEX, DOESN'T STAY OR WANT TO HUG UP AFTERWARDS
FUTURE	HE HAS HIS LIFE TOGETHER. HE HAS GOALS AND TALKS WITH YOU ABOUT THE FUTURE. YOU DISCUSS PLANS, HOPES DREAMS	HE RARELY TALKS ABOUT THE FUTURE. HE'S NOT REALLY ESTABLISHED, STILL TRYING TO FIND HIMSELF. YOU'RE NOT IN CONVERSATIONS PERTAINING TO HIS FUTURE. NOT SURE ABOUT HIS OWN FUTURE	NEVER DISCUSSES THE FUTURE. HE'S STILL TRYING TO "FIND HIMSELF" OR "GET HIMSELF TOGETHER" LIVES WITH HIS MOM OR OTHER PEOPLE DOESN'T HAVE HIS OWN HOUSE, APARTMENT, OR CAR. HAS NO CAREER GOALS

You know what I discovered? You can actually be your own kind of perfect and work in progress simultaneously.

Fabulous 5

Write down 5 things about yourself that you truly love

Write down 5 accomplishments you've achieved over the course of your life

Write down 5 things you are working on for self-improvement

Daily Motivation

"Your own kind of perfect & your work in progress is a lethal combination of badass & bold ass beautiful!!!!"

No matter how attractive a person is
in your mind of potential,
the fact is you have to date, communicate
and live in a relationship with their reality.
They will never ascend to your personal
expectation or vision.
What you see may not be what you really get
if you're looking at them
through the blinders of your mind.
Don't live in your relationship
with your eyes wide shut!

IN LOVE OR LIKE WITH THE PERSON OR THEIR POTENTIAL?

ARE YOU GLOSSING OVER THEIR FLAWS AND NOT VIEWING THEM FOR WHO THEY TRULY ARE?

DO YOU HOLD ON TO THE VISION OF WHO THEY KEEP SAYING THEY'RE HOPING TO BE, WITHOUT LOOKING AT WHO THEY TRULY ARE IN THE PRESENT?

ARE YOU MEETING THEM WHERE THEY ARE OR PULLING THEM INTO THE DESTINATION VACATION OF HOPE IN YOUR OWN MIND?

GETTING OUT OF THE HABIT OF FALLING FOR SOMEONE'S POTENTIAL REQUIRES CONSCIOUS THOUGHT. HERE ARE SOME SUGGESTIONS:

- STEP BACK AND REALLY LOOK AT WHO THEY TRULY ARE AND WHERE THEY ARE IN THE PRESENT.

- LOOK CLOSELY AT THE EFFORT AND WORK THEY ARE PUTTING IN TODAY.

- RECOGNIZE THE DIFFERENCE BETWEEN WHERE THEY ARE TRULY COMING FROM AND YOUR OWN EXPECTATION.

- LET GO OF THE DESIRE OR NEED TO CHANGE OR IMPROVE THEM.

- DON'T BECOME EMOTIONALLY VESTED BEFORE CLEARLY UNDERSTANDING THEIR TRUE INTENTIONS.

- DON'T ACCEPT OR APPLAUD THE BARE MINIMUM OR THINK THINGS LIKE BASIC RESPECT ARE SOMETHING EXTRA. BASELINE MINIMUM EFFORT ISN'T EXTRA SPECIAL.

- OBSERVE THEIR ACTIONS, AND BEHAVIORS LIKE BEING RELIABLE, ACCOUNTABLE, AND KEEPING THEIR WORD. WATCH CLOSELY HOW THEY SHOW UP IN YOUR LIFE.

- BE TOTALLY HONEST WITH YOURSELF AND ASK YOURSELF IF YOU ARE TRULY ABLE TO ACCEPT THIS PERSON FOR WHO THEY ARE BECAUSE THE CORE OF THE PERSON NEVER CHANGES. PEOPLE CAN BECOME BETTER PEOPLE BUT RARELY BECOME DIFFERENT PEOPLE.

- REMEMBER YOUR RELATIONSHIP AND YOUR PARTNER ARE NOT "DIY" PROJECTS THAT YOU CAN FIX UP, REPAIR, REHAB, OR MOLD INTO YOUR VERSION OR VIEW. IF YOU HAVE A HABIT OF ATTRACTING FIXER-UPPER PARTNERS, YOU PROBABLY HAVE SOME CONTROL ISSUES OR MAYBE YOU NEED TO FEEL SUPERIOR. SO, TAKE A LOOK IN THE MIRROR OF SELF-REFLECTION.

Nutrition Facts
Valeur nutritive
Per 1 cup (250 mL) / par 1 tasse (250 mL)

Amount   % Daily Value
Teneur   % valeur quotidienne
Calories / Calories 80
Fat / Lipides 0 g   0 %
 Saturated / saturés 0 g
 + Trans / trans 0 g   0 %
Cholesterol / Cholestérol 0 mg
Sodium / Sodium 115 mg   5 %
Carbohydrate / Glucides 18 g   4 %
 Fibre / Fibres 0 g   0 %
 Sugars / Sucres 11 g
Protein / Protéines 0 g
Vitamin A / Vitamine A   15 %
Vitamin C / Vitamine C   0 %
Calcium / Calcium   30 %
Iron / Fer   0 %
Vitamin D / Vitamine D   45 %

MAN OR WOMAN, THEM OR THEY, ONCE YOU FORGIVE YOUR SIGNIFICANT OTHER, LET THAT SHIT GO! STOP WARMING UP THE LEFTOVERS OF YOUR HURT OR DISAPPOINTMENT AND SERVING IT TO THEM FOR DINNER OVER AND OVER AGAIN.

IT HAS NO MORE NUTRITIONAL VALUE!

95

FORGIVE & MOVE FORWARD

GET A PACK OF DISSOLVING PAPER
(I FOUND MINE ON AMAZON)

WRITE A LETTER TO THOSE WHO HAVE HURT,
DISAPPOINTED, OR USED YOU. FILL THE LETTER
WITH ALL THE EMOTIONS, ANGER, SADNESS,
DISAPPOINTMENT, AND HEARTACHE THAT YOU
CAN. CURSE THEM OUT IF YOU NEED TO.

AT THE END OF YOUR LETTER WRITE THE
FOLLOWING:

I RELEASE ALL OF THE HURT, PAIN, ANGER AND
UNCOMFORTABLE FEELINGS THAT
_____ HAS CAUSED ME. I
FORGIVE FOR ME AND SET MYSELF FREE!

THEN PUT THE LETTER IN A JAR OF WARM WATER.
WATCH IT DISSOLVE AND LET YOUR NEGATIVE
FEELINGS DISSOLVE WITH IT. THEN POUR IT
DOWN THE DRAIN OR TOILET AND LET IT GO!

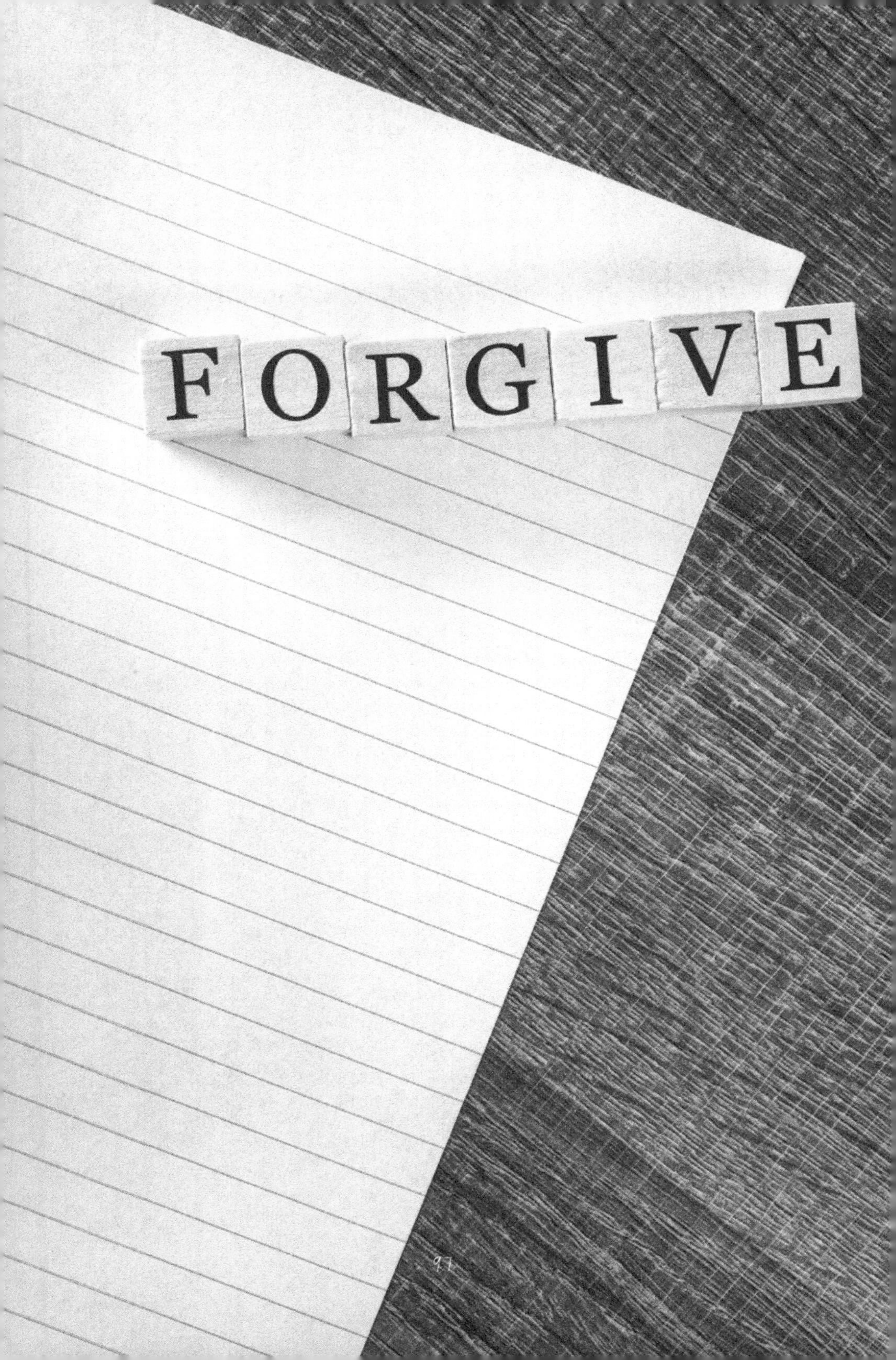
FORGIVE

If you plant your seeds on artificial turf, no matter how much you water it, nothing will ever grow. Make sure you are planting yourself in healthy soil you beautiful flower!

PLANTING SEEDS

In what type of environment do you want to plant your seeds?

What seeds are you planting in your life?

Will they grow in the environment in which you are planting them?

NEVER PLANT WHERE NOTHING GROWS!

You can't be the leading lady in your life's script if you keep allowing yourself to be a supporting actress. Make them choose you or lose you!
You're a headliner not an understudy!

Every Weekday
Starting June 1, 2022
Self Love Road

123 Headliner St., Never the understudy City

100

HEADLINER

WHAT QUALITIES MAKE YOU A HEADLINER OR LEADING LADY IN YOUR RELATIONSHIP?

_____

_____

_____

_____

_____

_____

_____

_____

_____

_____

_____

_____

_____

_____

_____

_____

_____

REMEMBER THIS...
IF THERE ARE OTHER WOMEN CONSTANTLY AUDITIONING FOR
THE ROLE,
FIND A NEW PART IN A NEW MOVIE WITH A
NEW LEADING MAN.

BAGGAGE

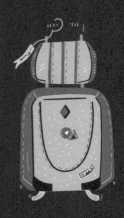

OVER MY 53 YEARS OF
LIVING, VALUABLE
LESSONS HAVE BEEN
MASTERED.
I'VE LEARNED TO
UNDERSTAND THAT WE
ARE NEVER BAGGAGE
THAT SOMEONE GETS
TIRED OF.
WE ARE SIMPLY COMPLEX
STORIES WITH HEAVY
EMOTIONAL BAGGAGE
THAT NOT EVERY SPINE
IS STRONG ENOUGH TO
CARRY.

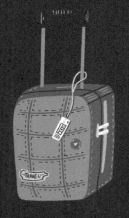

WHAT'S IN YOUR BAGS? ARE THEY STRONG ENOUGH TO CARRY IT?
WRITE ON EACH BAG WHAT EMOTIONAL BAGGAGE YOU MAY BE CARRYING IN YOUR RELATIONSHIP

IF YOU ARE READY TO UNPACK IT, LEAVE IT RIGHT HERE!

Mastering your own orgasms is somewhere in between a climactic destination vacation, sipping top shelf margaritas and nirvana. Neither requires another individual to enjoy it! "BOY BYE"

ME, MYSELF & I

Relationship Status

☐ Married

☐ Single

☑ IN A FULL-BLOWN RELATIONSHIP WITH ME, MYSELF & I

Being alone doesn't have to be lonely

List 10 things you enjoy doing alone

_____

_____

_____

_____

_____

_____

_____

_____

_____

_____

_____

_____

_____

_____

_____

_____

_____

_____

_____

**IN THOSE MOMENTS WHERE YOU NEED TO REGROUP OR FIND YOURSELF OR YOUR CENTER,
COME BACK TO THIS PAGE AND PICK SOMETHING TO DO FROM YOUR LIST**

Many people are uncomfortable doing things alone. They may challenge you to step out of your comfort zone. Doing things alone can be incredibly empowering. While conventional things you can do alone like, getting a pedicure, going to the movies, doing some yoga, or binge-watching Netflix is cool, try stepping out of the box occasionally. Below are a few unconventional suggestions you may want to try doing all by your amazingly wonderful self!

Racetrack Drive/Ride: Book a driving or riding experience on a racetrack in a Muscle-car like a McLaren, Ferrari, Lamborghini, or Bugatti. They will either teach you how to drive it or you can sit as a passenger. It's definitely an adrenaline rush. Then you can cross "Drive an exotic car" or "Drive a racecar" off you're your bucket list while embracing your solo time as well.

Go to a museum: Going to a museum alone gives you some good visual stimuli. You can walk through at your own pace and set your own itinerary. Museums can be tranquil but educational. I prefer art museums because I like losing myself in the colors. I'm oblivious to everyone else around me when I'm in my imagination. Going at least one time to a museum alone is something everyone should experience.

Take a dance class: Dance is a universal language that can be mastered all alone. Sign up for a salsa, tap, or hip-hop class. I prefer belly dancing or pole dancing classes because it challenges me to hit those moves. Whatever dance you like, doing it alone is never lonely.

Volunteer: Clinicians know there's a healing power to touch, especially for Premature babies or those born with addiction or other health problems. So, volunteering as a baby rocker or cuddler can be rewarding not just for the infants but also for you. There's no feeding involved, changing diapers, or involvement in any medical care. You don't even need to walk around with them. You simply hold the babies, read, sing, or talk, while rocking them. It's therapeutic for the infant as well as for you. Studies have shown that people who volunteer as rockers or cuddlers have improved brain function, reduced depression, and increased feelings of happiness.

If he's the king of mixed signals don't become the queen of getting your hopes up! Mixed signals are clear messages, and that message is probably no!

EXAMPLES OF MIXED SIGNALS

- Takes a long time to reply to texts or infrequently texts.
- They run hot and cold. One minute he's all over you, the next minute he seems to be avoiding you.
- Says he's not ready for a relationship but still keeps asking you out.
- He doesn't want to make it official, but he acts jealous of other men.
- Doesn't show affection to you in public but knocks your back out in the bedroom.
- He leaves you on "READ" when you're in a mid-text conversation, then you see "read" and no follow-up.
- You go out, the date went well as far as you could tell, then he doesn't call or message you for several days.

DECIPHERING THE CODE

- HE TEXTS YOU SOMETHING PRETTY MEANINGLESS OR SIMPLE "WYD" "HEY" "HI" OR "WHAT'S UP" AFTER YOU HAVEN'T HEARD FROM HIM IN A FEW DAYS: HE WANTS TO SEE IF YOU'RE STILL FEELING HIM, AND HE IS FEELING YOU OUT TO SEE IF YOU ARE STILL AN OPTION OR AVAILABLE WHEN HE WANTS.
- YOU TALK OR TEXT PRETTY FREQUENTLY, BUT HE NEVER PLANS DATES WITH YOU, AND YOU NEVER REALLY GET TOGETHER OFTEN: HE LIKES CHATTING YOU UP, MAYBE ENJOYS YOUR CONVERSATIONS OR EVEN FLIRTING WITH YOU BUT THERE'S NO REAL CONNECTION FOR HIM.
- AFTER YOU HANG OUT OR HAVE SEX, HE GOES M.I.A. A FEW DAYS OR APPEARS TO BE ALWAYS BUSY: HE LIKELY IS SEEING SOMEONE ELSE.
- HE ONLY CALLS LATE AT NIGHT OR WANTS TO COME TO YOUR HOUSE AT NIGHT: HE IS PROBABLY ONLY PHYSICALLY ATTRACTED TO YOU. YOU'RE MOST LIKELY A BOOTY CALL AND HE'S NOT REALLY INTERESTED IN CONNECTING WITH YOU ON A DEEPER LEVEL OR SPENDING QUALITY TIME DATING YOU.

Sis... Stop letting these men spin the teacups, ride the roller-coaster and play skee-ball on your body! Your life is no amusement park!

- You shouldn't be in a relationship where you have to constantly buckle up because the ride is constantly up and down, upside-down, or round and round.

- Rushing into sex may leave you feeling regretful, empty, and out of control.

- Slow down before engaging in sex. Take your time so that you can get a better idea of whether or not you truly even like the person.

- Having sex too soon can send bad messages or mixed signals. He may feel sex is all you're looking for too. So, be conscious of what you are showing him.

- Remember men react more to their biological urges, so don't perceive sex as a love connection.

- Set the pace on cruise control to a slower speed. Pump your brakes! This isn't to play games but to get to know each other better and let the man do what he's supposed to do. That is "woo and pursue you." Men are hunters by nature, let them hunt. His primal instinct is to pursue. Men like to chase.

STOP CHASING AND MAKING YOURSELF AVAILABLE!

IF YOU KNOW
YOU ARE
CHAMPAGNE IN
A FLUTED
GLASS...
DON'T LET
ANYONE TREAT
YOU LIKE
WARM PISS IN
A PAPER CUP
OR FLAT BEER
IN A BONG!

114

Cheers to yourself!

Your champagne taste isn't made for everyone's palate. Today, go get yourself a bottle of champagne or some good sparkling cider, pour it into a pretty flute and have a bomb ass toast to your boss ass beautiful self!!!!!

List some things here about yourself that deserve a toast

Positivity Reminder

You can't have Louboutin expectations with a dollar store flip-flop mentality! So, level up and keep you heels high and your goals higher!

sonyaism

FLIP FLOP MENTALITY OR HIGH HEEL MIND

Stop accepting less when you know you deserve more

Just for today, even if you don't wear heels, put on a pair of kick-ass high heels and put your feet up on a footstool, table, or chair in front of you to remind you that you have high standards. If you don't have high heels or can't wear high heels, you can virtually borrow those pictured below.

Snap a picture of the shoes below and make it your screen saver for today or any other day. Use it as a reminder that you have high standards!

REMEMBER, THE ONLY TIME YOUR HEAD SHOULD EVER BE DOWN IS TO ADMIRE YOUR FABULOUS FOOTWEAR!

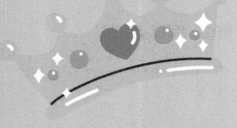

SOMETIMES THE CROWN YOU WEAR IS
FILLED WITH SO MANY PRICELESS
PRECIOUS JEWELS THAT IT'S TOO
HEAVY FOR THE AVERAGE MAN TO
CARRY YOU. THEN YOU DOWNSIZE TO
A SMALLER CROWN TO MAKE IT
EASIER FOR HIM TO CARRY...
GURLLLLLLL
YOU DON'T NEED A SMALLER CROWN!
YOU NEED A MAN WITH BIGGER HANDS
AND A STRONGER BACKBONE!!!
OH... AND AN EXTRA INCH!!

Are you wearing a crown, a tiara, a headband, or a dunce cap in your relationship?

JUST FOR TODAY, STOP AND THANK YOURSELF FOR HOW FAR YOU HAVE COME, THE PROGRESS YOU HAVE MADE AND ALL THAT YOU ARE. NO, IT HASN'T BEEN EASY, BUT YOU HAVE BEEN WORTH IT!

THANK YOU

I did, I can, I will

Name one thing you never thought you would survive or get over

What tools, strategies or practices helped you to move forward?

How can you use those same methods to help you get over your situationship/relationship?

When you can build the table, buy the table, set the table and bring all of your kickass in a shot glass, along with your badass & beautiful sass to the table... you better not be begging for a seat at anyone else's table!

10 THINGS A PARTNER SHOULD PROBABLY BRING TO THE TABLE

1. ENCOURAGEMENT

2. SUPPORT

3. GREAT SEX PAIRED WITH INTIMACY

4. A SENSE OF SECURITY, SUPPORT AND SAFETY

5. GOALS, ASPIRATIONS AND PLANS

6. AMBITION

7. WILLINGNESS TO SHARE

8. ENGAGING CONVERSATION

9. LOYALTY

10. TRUST

My Table

What top 10 things do you bring to the table?

(Now before you roll out that long list of things like degrees, credit scores, and a salary, which are all great accomplishments, take a moment to think about things that cannot be earned, bought, or achieved). Now answer the question.

Has it ever occurred to you that you are the whole package that may simply be at the wrong address?
When you've been delivered to the wrong address you will be mishandled because they don't know what to do with you and they weren't meant to receive you in the first place!
The wrong person only wants part of you.
The right person wants and values the entire package!

WHAT'S IN YOUR PACKAGE?

WRITE IN THE BOXES BELOW WHAT MAKES YOU THE WHOLE PACKAGE WORTH KEEPING

If your **eyes** stay wet more
than your panties
and the **tears** ruin your
mascara more than the
kisses ruin your lipstick  ...
Sugarlicious you are in the
wrong relationship!

How many times in the past 30 days have you been intimately kissed?

How many times in the past 30 days have you had intimate conversations?

How many times in the past 30 days have you had a romantic dinner?

How many times have you cried or been upset about your relationship in the past 30 days?

SO, IS YOUR LIPSTICK SMEARING MORE THAN YOUR MASCARA IS RUNNING?

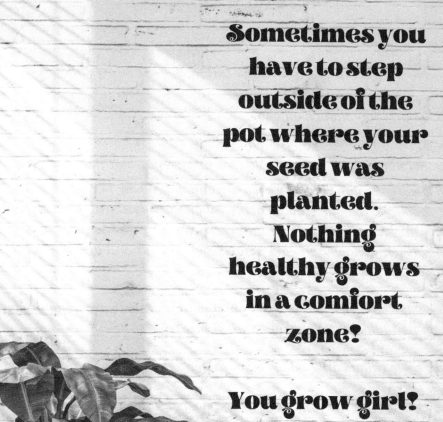

Sometimes you have to step outside of the pot where your seed was planted. Nothing healthy grows in a comfort zone!

You grow girl!

COMFORT ZONE

5 Activities to Get You Out of Your Comfort Zone

1. Do a 7-day plank challenge.
2. Make a decision by tossing a coin and just leave it to chance.
3. Try a new food you don't like or think you won't like.
4. Embrace your youth by reconnecting with your inner child. Go swing at the park, do a cartwheel or slide down the slide or ride your kid's tricycle down the street.
5. Put your shower on cold before stepping out and breathe through it.

Pick your own "get out of your comfort zone" challenges and apply them periodically throughout your life.

What one thing can you do today to get out of your comfort zone?

Being uncomfortable sparks growth and change.

Some people expect you
to shrink to be digestible.
They don't wanna chew
and swallow the entire
donut, so they expect you
to become the hole.
You are a beautiful,
glazed donut or a luscious
cinnamon bun, and if they
don't like the sweet
sugary comforting carb
that you are...
Tell them to go choke on
one of those empty-
tasting protein puffs!

Stop Shrinking!

Ways to make your presence larger

- Make eye contact
- Let go of the past
- Set boundaries
- Speak up
- Invest in yourself
- Stop saying sorry unless you are truly apologizing
- Wear a hot, sexy outfit
- Stop accommodating others at your own expense
- Say no to things you don't want to do or cannot commit to and don't apologize
- Do a 5-point Yoga spread. This is a strong power posture that forces you to take up more space. Try to do this every morning upon rising to start your day large and in charge
- Speak up and speak out with confidence
- Say, "It's time for me to choose myself!"
- Walk in your own authority
- Be your authentic self
- Don't seek validation from anyone or anything

The most powerful way to take up more space is to
VALUE YOURSELF
Know that just by being you, just by being yourself
you already add value to the world.
Take your rightful space up in this world.
YOU ARE WORTHY OF IT!

Remember that "NO" is a complete sentence all by itself
No follow up is required
There are also various creative ways to say NO
These are the hard NOs

- Nah dawg
- I'm good
- No thanks
- Nope
- Hell to the nah
- Uhhhh...yeah...NO
- Absolutely not!
- Not!
- Thanks but no thanks

NO DOESN'T HAVE TO BE HARD
THERE ARE SUBTLE SOFTER WAYS TO SAY NO LIKE THE SAMPLES BELOW

- I'm not ready for this
- I'm unable to commit to that
- Unfortunately I'll have to pass on that
- Thank you but it's not a viable option for me
- I'd rather not
- I'd prefer not to
- I have prior commitments
- That's not in alignment with my needs

I'm saying NO!

What are you tolerating today but not really feeling or interested in?

_____

_____

_____

_____

What will you not tolerate in your life?

_____

_____

_____

_____

What will you not tolerate in your relationship?

_____

_____

_____

_____

_____

SAY NO TO SOMETHING TODAY!

You could give some people a single drop of water
and they would be grateful, loyal, and sincerely appreciate you.
Then there are people you could give the entire ocean
and they will still take you for granted, play you, be ungrateful,
and have no loyalty.
Keep the ocean for yourself and keep sharing your drops with
those that appreciate you and show you that you matter!

WHO APPRECIATES YOU IN YOUR LIFE?

Write their names on the drops of water.
Draw more drops if you like.
When you feel unappreciated, come back to this page to remind you of
those who appreciate you.

BE KIND TO Yourself

Don't beat yourself up because you've spent your time fighting to hold on to a relationship with an individual who wasn't capable of reciprocating the love, respect, and encouragement you had to offer. Don't ever feel humiliated or ashamed of loving.

You saw something in them they couldn't see in themselves.

You saw their potential.

That does not make you stupid.

It simply makes you a victim of your own optimism.

Your beautiful superpower of seeing the better in them when they can't even see it themselves is a gift, not a curse.

EVERYONE HAS A PURPOSE IN YOUR LIFE
EVEN THOSE WHO HURT YOU, PLAYED YOU OR USED YOU
SO, IF THEY TOOK YOU ON EMOTIONAL ROLLERCOASTER RIDES,
DISRUPTED YOUR PEACE, HURT YOU, OR DISRESPECTED YOU
THEY WERE THE BEST TEACHERS OF HOW TO USE THE GIFT OF
INTUITION AND HOW TO READ BAD ENERGY
THEY TAUGHT YOU HOW TO READ BAD VIBES AND HELPED
CREATE YOUR LIST OF THINGS THAT YOU DO NOT WANT IN
YOUR LIFE
WHEN YOU MOVE ON, SMILING YOUR HAPPY, BOSS-ASS OFF,
YOU TAUGHT THEM WHAT SELF-LOVE LOOKS LIKE AND THAT
YOU ARE POWERFUL ENOUGH TO HEAL YOUR OWN WOUNDS

IT WASN'T A LOSS... IT WAS A LESSON!

Lesson of the day!

My Lessons

Write the lessons you learned from your past relationships

(Example: the biggest lesson in my own failed relationships was if I don't love myself enough, I will be chasing for love in all the wrong places, in all the wrong people, and all the wrong faces)

I learned...

_____

_____

_____

_____

_____

_____

_____

_____

_____

_____

_____

_____

_____

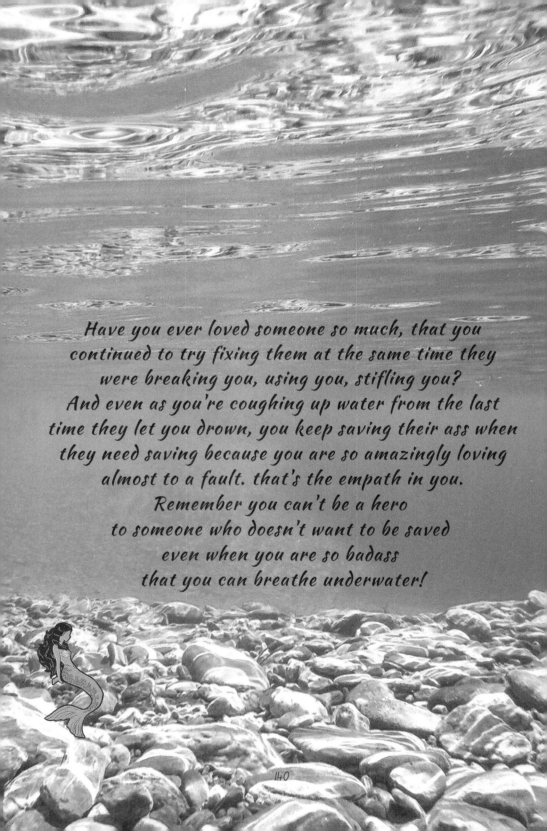

Have you ever loved someone so much, that you
continued to try fixing them at the same time they
were breaking you, using you, stifling you?
And even as you're coughing up water from the last
time they let you drown, you keep saving their ass when
they need saving because you are so amazingly loving
almost to a fault. that's the empath in you.
Remember you can't be a hero
to someone who doesn't want to be saved
even when you are so badass
that you can breathe underwater!

Self Care Routine

Put On Your own O2 Mask

Self-Care is essential!
You must always
put your own oxygen mask on first!

Take the pledge of Self-Care today and
say out loud:
"I PLEDGE TO PUT ON MY OWN OXYGEN
MASK FIRST!"

Right now, shift away from always
DOING to simply BEING present. Give
yourself permission to breathe then
look at your breath as an act of taking
in all that is available for you in the
moment and then exhale as a release
and act of surrender.

In this state of BEING, just for two or three minutes simply BREATHE.
Not your normal everyday inhaling of necessary O2, but a deliberate
purposeful deep breath and awareness of your intake of air.
For this two or three minutes, worry about nothing and worry about
no one. It's YOUR moment. You matter!

GO AHEAD AND TEST MY WATERS IF YOU WANT TO!
YOU BETTER COME WITH A RAFT, A LIFE VEST, AND AN OXYGEN TANK!
YOU MAY ALSO NEED TO NOT ONLY BE ABLE TO SWIM
BUT TO ALSO BREATHE UNDERWATER!

I'M NOT A FISH IN A FISHBOWL BRUH!
I'M A SHARK LIVING IN THE WHOLE ENTIRE OCEAN!

Sonyaism

142

Fishbowl Mentality

If you put a fish in a bowl or tank, it stops growing after a certain size relative to the size of the bowl. In a larger natural habitat, the fish will continue to grow. We often stay small in small environments out of habit. That includes staying in relationships even when there is no growth.

If you feel stifled and unable to grow in your relationship, maybe it's time to jump out of the fishbowl and into the sea of prospects, potential and amazing possibilities.

You will never know the depth or beauty of the ocean if you never leave your fishbowl and dive into the sea.

GETTING OUT OF THE FISHBOWL

In the fishbowl below, write the things, thoughts, and people that may be keeping you in the fishbowl and not allowing you to grow

In the ocean below write down things that will help you grow

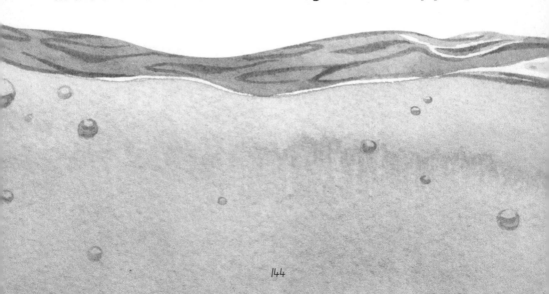

THE RELATIONSHIP TRAFFIC LIGHT

This exercise can be used to assess your significant other as well as yourself

Color in the corresponding circles that apply to your significant other or yourself. If something doesn't apply or you don't really know, do not color in the circle at all

If you have more red lights: **STOP!**

(This is an unhealthy relationship probably not worth saving)

If you have more green Lights: **GO!**

(This is most likely a healthy, viable relationship & worth the effort)

If you have more yellow lights: **CAUTION!**

(Slow down, take caution & wait before proceeding)

Keep in mind your traffic light outline may look very different than what is outlined

We each have unique requirements for our relationships

I listed this outline based on things I thought might be the most common or relevant

So, feel free to swap out the behaviors for the ones that you see fit or create your own traffic light list

YOUR LIFE, YOUR RULES, YOUR CHOICES!

YOU ARE THE AUTHOR OF YOUR OWN STORY!

YOU ARE THE INVENTOR OF YOUR OWN TRAFFIC LIGHTS IN YOUR AMAZING LIFE JOURNEY!

RED LIGHT SIGNALS

- Addiction
- Cheater or Liar
- Abuse (physical, emotional, or financial)
- Overly jealous or controlling
- Stands you up or cancels often
- Selfish and only concerned about their own wants, needs, and desires
- Bullies you or others
- Is in a relationship (Married, lives together, or engaged)
- You find yourself sad or crying often about the way they treat you
- Doesn't value you, treats you like an option
- You're mostly a booty call
- Doesn't plan or take you on dates
- Doesn't travel with you
- Avoids ever discussing your future
- Not open to change or suggestions
- Calls you crazy, stupid, lazy, or other derogatory names
- Doesn't really like you
- Makes or expects you to do things that you don't feel comfortable doing
- Hates your family or close friends
- Can't keep a job or lacks ambition
- Makes excuses for their behavior or their life or blames everyone else for their problems

YELLOW LIGHT SIGNALS

- Messy or unorganized
- Problems showing emotion or vulnerability
- Has children from prior relationships
- Not great at managing money
- Struggles communicating
- Impatient
- Difficulty making decisions
- Low credit score
- You're unsure about your feelings
- Has "mama's boy" tendencies
- Can appear too flirty or too chatty with others
- Difficulty managing money
- Previously married
- Never been in a committed relationship
- They have no close friends
- They have a bad relationship or no relationship with their mother or father
- They don't want or don't really like children

GREEN LIGHT SIGNALS

- You usually feel happy in their company
- You feel safe in your relationship
- They compliment you and celebrate your success or accomplishments
- You enjoy spending time with them, but also enjoy your time apart
- They don't judge you or try to control you
- You feel appreciated and you appreciate them
- They are responsible and reliable and keep their word
- You share common interests and goals
- They notice the little things like a new outfit, hairstyle, nails, favorite color, etc.
- You have good engaging conversations
- You communicate well and have healthy arguments that result in resolution
- Not afraid to apologize or admit when they are wrong
- They have goals & aspirations
- Good work ethic
- Remembers important events (birthdays, holidays, special occasions)
- You have a lot in common
- You have a lot of intimacy (not just sex)
- You can be yourself around them and feel comfortable
- They stand up for you or defend your honor
- They are fun, spontaneous
- They give you that warm fuzzy feeling or satisfy your sweet spots

NOW COUNT YOUR COLORED CIRCLES & COLOR IN THE TRAFFIC LIGHT THAT HAD THE MOST.
TOP LIGHT RED, MIDDLE LIGHT YELLOW, BOTTOM LIGHT GREEN.

IS IT TIME TO STOP, WAIT OR GO FORWARD?

IF YOU'VE DECIDED TO STAY IN YOUR SIDECHICKUATIONSHIP THEN PLAY BY THE RULES!

SIDECHICKUATIONSHIP CODE OF CONDUCT

1. **Stay in your lane/know your role:** You have no authority, and you don't make the rules. You have no rights in his life.
2. **Do not disturb:** Do not bother, confront, or disrupt his wife or main chick. You cannot stalk, harass or threaten him with talk of telling her. Don't stalk her on social media trying to find out what she looks like, if she's educated, or who her friends are.
3. **Do not fall in love:** Once you become too emotional, the way he moves with you will change.
4. **You must keep yourself available:** He's the one making most of the decisions.
5. **Stay under the radar:** If you run into him with his family or friends, go with the flow that he outlines.
6. **No leaving evidence:** No matter how tired you may be of the Sidechickuationship, no leaving lipstick, hair, or perfume on his person, on his things, or in his car. Some side chicks play that game and leave things purposely. Big NO-NO!
7. **Retain social media silence:** No pictures of him on your page, no selfies with him, no pics taken inside his car. No tagging on Facebook or liking things he posts on Instagram. In fact, it's advisable to not follow him on any social media platforms. Social media etiquette is a must!
8. **Your sex game face and fun face should be on at all times:** Your job is to please him so be ready for sex whenever and wherever. Don't ask questions. Remember your time with him is the only time that he's really your business.
9. **Never forget:** The wife/main chick will always come first.
10. **You are the personal assistant:** Not the boss.

STAYING IN YOUR SITUATIONSHIP

Being single may frustrate you. Being alone may at times frighten you. But being in an unhealthy, unfulfilling, or bad relationship that does not allow growth or progression will damage you!

Some people actually prefer a Situationship over a committed relationship and that's perfectly fine if it works for all parties involved. Maybe commitment is not in cards for the moment. Maybe it can't be because of various circumstances. Either way, if you've decided to stay that's your choice. After all, as adults, we have the right to make our own choices.

No matter what your reason is for staying, keep in mind that there are pros and cons to all Situationships. The pros might be there's no pressure and you have more freedom. However, the cons could be potentially losing a good friend if it ends badly or possibly missing out on the connection to the love of your life because you missed it while playing the untitled role in your Situationship. Pros and cons vary based on what you personally feel. Determining if a Situationship is good for you still takes an internal assessment of what you deem acceptable or not.

But if you've planted your feet in your Situationship and you don't mind riding the wave of ambiguity, there are still suggested rules even though there are technically no rules in a Situationship.

THE SUGGESTED RULES ARE AS FOLLOWS:

- **Stay in your lane:** You have no rights to the other piece of your Situationship's life. You have no authority. So, you cannot be upset if they don't consider you in making decisions in their life. For example, if they decide to fly off to Belize with another friend, you shouldn't be upset or confront them about it because you aren't exclusive. If they text someone in the middle of the night, while lying on the left side of your bed, you have no say so.

- **Do not catch feelings:** If they post pics hugged up on Instagram or make a TikTok video dancing with another person, keep your emotions in check. If they take someone else to their cousin's wedding and didn't invite you to come, you shouldn't be mad or jealous once you've committed to the non-commitment. Don't be upset when they spend time with anyone else.

- **Expect Nothing:** Don't expect more than what's being given. If they typically see you only on Thursday, don't start expecting, Friday and Saturday too. If they don't typically make plans and you've been scheduling movie times or dinner dates, don't expect them to take the wheel if that's how it started.

- **If you ever change your mind, make your needs, or wants clear:** Don't keep straddling the fence playing like you're still ok with the Situationship if your emotions have kicked in and you want something more. Know when it's time to have the DTR (Define The Relationship) or have the WITUG (Where Is This Ultimately Going) conversation. Don't expect your partner to be a mind reader. If you've been rolling along in the non-strings attached Situationship and your feelings have changed let the other person know. Don't blindside them with a whole lot of drama and emotional overload. The game never changes, but people do.

STAYING IN ANY RELATIONSHIP

Deciding whether or not you should stay in your Situationship or relationship is a personal choice. It depends on your circumstances at that time, core values, what a healthy relationship looks like to you, and what your long-term goals may be. You should figure out at some point in your life if you want to be married someday, or if you plan on staying single. After all, marriage is not something that is on everyone's "To Do List". Marriage is a personal choice.

Determine if you need monogamy in your partner or if polyamorous connections work better for you. What people define as healthy relationships are not always built on the foundation of monogamy. Healthy relationships are strictly built on personal preference. But healthiness in any type of relationship starts with clear, concise communication on what the expectation is as well as respect and honesty.

Healthy relationships have a universal common denominator which is that it makes you feel good. If it makes you feel sad, mad, confused, or unsure, it's not healthy so it may not work in your favor. Figuring out what you want or even don't want is the key to a healthy decision on staying or going. If you're not ready to settle and the Situationship is working well for you, feel free to stay, play and make the most of it to your benefit. However, if you want different things or your partner wants to take things to a new or different level, it's advisable to walk away from the Situationship before it becomes toxic. If you don't end the Situationship then, it morphs into a Toxicuationship.

No matter what the status of your relationship is or what term you use to define it, the staying rules are relatively the same. Whether you're married, engaged, living together, boyfriend & girlfriend, girlfriend & girlfriend, boyfriend & boyfriend, them & them, they & they, the basis is similar.

- Know what you want and what you don't want: Figure out what you are both willing to accept or not accept.

- Recognize healthy relationships: Any relationship in your life should feel like a soft sweet spot. Though healthy may not be a committed one in the traditional sense or may not be monogamous, the core elements like trust, respect and open communication should be the foundation.

- Remember you can always at any point and time in your life, change your mind: Our needs and desires change continuously. Just be willing to communicate your feelings when the relationship expectations change so you can be on the same page.

THE DO'S TO NOT LOSING YOURSELF OR FINDING YOURSELF

We all have at some point lost ourselves in a relationship. There are a variety of things in our lives that contribute to losing ourselves. Things like dysfunctional families, low self-esteem, toxic people or toxic energy in our spaces, past trauma, or heavy social media influences. So, the practice of self-care is essential to not losing yourself. It's a beautiful thing to be a great wife, mom, friend, sister, auntie, or employee but it's more important to be your beautiful true, authentic SELF.

- Do be you
- Do give them space
- Do retain your authenticity
- Do stay in contact with your true friends
- Do set boundaries
- Do remember your passions and purpose
- Do date yourself
- Do take care of yourself
- Do treat yourself to some pampering
- Do try new things
- Do love yourself first
- Do remember and know your value
- Do stay spiritually grounded
- Do take responsibility for your own happiness
- Do work on your relationship with yourself as a priority

I know why some of the most beautiful dope women
are still single and turning down prospects...
it's not because they are hard to love!
it's not because they are too picky!
it's not because they aren't enough!

It's because what they want is rare
and because they refuse to settle for
less than what they have rightfully
decided that they deserve!

REMINDER

Even a booty call should demand some
level of engaging conversation.
Your mind and heart deserve just as
much attention if not more than your
lady parts!

Decline	Accept

66 Ladies, stop playing wife to a
boyfriend, a booty call or
a friend-with-benefits!
He will never put a ring on it or give
you his last name if you haven't made
it a requirement!
A ring won't save your relationship
neither will a baby or 2 babies or more
Oh... and neither will a threesome!!! **99**

It's ok if I'm not your cup
of tea
I'm too busy being a
bottle of 1945 Romanee
Conti

Yeah, there's a lot of fish in the sea, but it's rare you'll catch a mermaid!

sonyaism

If you stop setting places at your table for people who don't appreciate what's being served, your meals will become much more peaceful.

The purpose of this survival guide is not only to recognize and navigate through Situationships or relationships with other people. It serves as a reminder to ultimately get into the mindset that the most important relationship is the one that you have with yourself. Self-Love, Self-Care, and Self-Worth are the foundations of any relationship with anyone. We always hear that relationships require work. This is often interpreted to mean that our personal relationships, romantic relationships, or any relationship with others need our attention and work. While it's partially true, our relationship with ourselves requires the most attention. When we think about the relationships that are most important to us, we often neglect to consider the once we have with ourselves. The tone for how you show up in any other relationship is set by the relationship you have with yourself.

BELOW ARE FIVE THINGS I DO CONSISTENTLY THAT HAVE BEEN USEFUL IN HAVING A BETTER RELATIONSHIP WITH MYSELF AND PRACTICING SELF-CARE

True love is YOU love! You have to choose and love yourself first always

1. **Walk barefoot on the earth:** It can be the grass, the ground, the sand, or the dirt, wherever and whenever you have a space to plant your feet on the earth is therapeutic. Doing this can neutralize your energy. Walking barefoot on the earth allows you to release any negative energy that you may be carrying into the earth. That's where you are allowed to plant it. If you can do this daily that's great. If you can't, try it at least once per week.

2. **Meditate/pray daily:** I find this to be one of the best gifts to oneself. Engaging in some sort of daily spiritual practice can still the mind and carry us through stressful moments, heavy days, and overwhelming thoughts.

3. **Daily affirmations:** Doing this allows me to quiet my inner critic. I tend to at times be overly critical of myself, so I have to minimize the negative self-talk. It helps me to remember to be kind to myself.

4. **Journal daily:** Journaling helps me be aware of where I am mentally and emotionally each day. Putting my thoughts down on paper helps me reflect. I also use journaling for "brain dumping." If you're unfamiliar with the term, a brain dump is a chance to get everything out of your head and onto some paper. This helps create more space in my overthinking head.

5. **Practice conscious deliberate breathing:** Paying attention to your breath anchors and stabilizes you. Taking five or ten minutes each day to simply inhale and exhale purposefully improves functions of the nervous system and respiratory system filling the brain with oxygen. Learning to do deep diaphragmic breathing has a host of benefits to your physical and mental health.

SELFCARE BINGO

Use a pencil (so you can erase and reuse this page) and track your self-care activities by crossing off an activity for the day. Only cross off one per day even if you do more. The goal is to get at least once BINGO row completed in any direction. After you've achieved a BINGO, reward yourself with something. How about a massage, facial, foot reflexology, a new pair of kicks (shoes or sneakers), a piece of chocolate, an ice cream cone, a love letter to yourself. Whatever you decide, you deserve, because you took care of YOU!

pray or meditate	took a nap	exercised	breathed deliberately	relaxed
went social media free for a day	paid it forward	brain dumped	journaled	drank 1/2 your body weight in water
asked for help	said no to something	**FREE SPACE!**	had a good night's sleep	said positive affirmations
exercised or danced	got some shit done	ate something healthy	finished something	exercised
tried something new	made my bed	write your own	write your own	write your own

BRAIN DUMP

Write out your thoughts in no particular order in the big box first then go back and place them in the applicable worth boxes.

CURRENT STATE OF MIND:

◯ OVERWHELMED ◯ OVERJOYED ◯ OVER IT

WORTH IT	WORTH CONSIDERING	NOT WORTH IT

DEAL WITH THE THINGS IN YOUR WORTH IT BOX FIRST

THERE ARE MANY SITES ONLINE OFFERING FREE BRAIN DUMP TEMPLATES AND EXERCISES, SO GOOGLE IS YOUR FRIEND.

REMEMBER THIS:

Remember the most important relationship is the one that you have with yourself. So, YOU are your priority. Whether you are married, single, divorced, testing the waters, in a relationship or situationship, navigating and staying afloat relies heavily on your self-care routines, your level of self-love and how much you value yourself. I hope you rise and thrive because you will surely survive!

CONCLUSION

It's my hope that you found this book fun, empowering, enlightening and a source of thought-provoking reminders. We all have had probably at least one relationship or Situationship challenge. So the intent in writing this was to help navigate the complexities of various relationships in an interactive and lovingly big-sister type of way. The most important things I hope people take away from this book are as follows:

- An understanding of the importance of not losing yourself in a relationship
- Recognizing and dealing with healthy vs. unhealthy relatioships
- Knowing your worth and that you are valuable
- You don't have to settle for anything less than you deserve
- Whether it's a situationship or full-blown relationship, you have the right to decide how it moves, how it ends, or how it stays afloat

Sonya Manuel, the author of Situationships Are Full of Situationshit, grew up in Orange, New Jersey where she spent most of her youth buried in pages of books at the local library. As a result of becoming a self-proclaimed bibliophile, her love of books developed into a love for writing. While most of her writing over the years has been technical writing in her Health Information Management career, she never lost her passion for writing books and helping others. Her writing is sassy and filled with passion. She's like the big sister who hugs you, protects you, and fights for you but kicks you in the ass when needed. She writes with the hope to help people heal their own wounds, empower their lives and be their authentic selves.

She's been described by many as a "Saucy-Scintillating Spitfire" and the "Postess with the Mostess" on her social media.

She once described herself and her writing style as "kickass in a shot glass of realism, meditating in Zen stilettos."

"Over my 53 years of living, valuable lessons have been mastered.
I've learned to understand that we are never baggage that someone gets tired of...
We are simply complex stories with heavy emotional baggage that not every spine is strong enough to carry"

Made in the USA
Columbia, SC
03 August 2022

64502293R00098